my **revision** notes

Cambridge National Level 1/2

INFORMATION TECHNOLOGIES

Sonia Stuart

HODDER
EDUCATION
AN HACHETTE UK COMPANY

The Publishers would like to thank the following for permission to reproduce copyright material.

Photo credits

P.7 © zadorozhna/stock.adobe.com; p.27 © Andrey Popov/stock.adobe.com; p.28 © Washington Imaging/Alamy Stock Photo; p.29 © Realimage/Alamy Stock Photo; p.33 *m* © toons17/stock.adobe.com; p.34 *t* © phoelixDE/Shutterstock, *b* © sdecoret/stock.adobe.com; p.36 *t* © Jerome Dancett/Fotolia, *m* © istockphoto/Oleksiy Mark , *b* ©brentmelissa/istockphoto; p.37 © Xuejun li/Fotolia; p.39 *t* © DaiPhoto/stock.adobe.com, *b* © Alice_photo/stock.adobe.com; p.41 © dclic-photo.fr/stock.adobe.com; p.42 © Fenton – Fotolia; p.53 © Peter Widmann/Alamy Stock Photo; p.60 © kevma20/stock.adobe.com; p.61 © B Christopher/Alamy Stock Photo; p.76 © Justin Kase zsixz/Alamy Stock Photo; p.82 © nattanan/stock.adobe.com; p.84 © WavebreakmediaMicro/stock.adobe.com.

Although every effort has been made to ensure that website addresses are correct at time of going to press, Hodder Education cannot be held responsible for the content of any website mentioned in this book. It is sometimes possible to find a relocated web page by typing in the address of the home page for a website in the URL window of your browser.

Hachette UK's policy is to use papers that are natural, renewable and recyclable products and made from wood grown in well-managed forests and other controlled sources. The logging and manufacturing processes are expected to conform to the environmental regulations of the country of origin.

Orders: please contact Hachette UK Distribution, Hely Hutchinson Centre, Milton Road, Didcot, Oxfordshire, OX11 7HH. Telephone: +44 (0)1235 827827. Email education@hachette.co.uk. Lines are open from 9 a.m. to 5 p.m., Monday to Friday. You can also order through our website: www.hoddereducation.co.uk.

ISBN: 978 1 5104 2328 2

© Sonia Stuart 2018

First published in 2018 by
Hodder Education,
An Hachette UK Company
Carmelite House
50 Victoria Embankment
London EC4Y 0DZ

www.hoddereducation.co.uk

Impression number 10 9 8 7 6

Year 2026 2025 2024 2023 2022 2021

Cover photo © royyimzy – stock.adobe.com

Typeset in India

Printed in India

A catalogue record for this title is available from the British Library.

Get the most from this book

Everyone has to decide his or her own revision strategy, but it is essential to review your work, learn it and test your understanding. These Revision Notes will help you do that in a planned way, topic by topic. Use this book as the cornerstone of your revision and don't hesitate to write in it: personalise your notes and check your progress by ticking off each section as you revise.

Tick to track your progress

Use the revision planner on pages 4 and 5 to plan your revision, topic by topic. Tick each box when you have:

- revised and understood a topic
- tested yourself
- practised the exam questions and checked your answers.

You can also keep track of your revision by ticking off each topic heading in the book. You may find it helpful to add your own notes as you work through each topic.

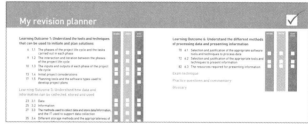

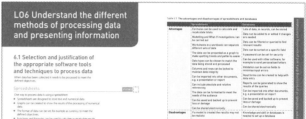

Features to help you succeed

My revision planner

Learning Outcome 6: Understand the different methods of processing data and presenting information

Exam technique

Practice questions and commentary

Glossary

LO1 Understand the tools and techniques that can be used to initiate and plan solutions

1.1 The phases of the project life cycle and the tasks carried out in each phase

1.1.1 The phases of the project life cycle

REVISED

There are four phases of the project life cycle:

- Initiation
- Planning
- Execution
- Evaluation.

Each phase has tasks that must be completed before the next phase can be started.

Table 1.1 Tasks to be completed during each phase

Phase	Tasks
Initiation	Gather user requirements and constraints from client
	Define success criteria and objectives
	Consider legislative implications
	Create feasibility report
	Complete phase review
Planning	Define constraints
	Create project plans and resource lists
	Produce initial designs
	Create test plans
	Complete phase review
Execution	Use project plan to monitor project
	Create deliverable product
	Test deliverable product
	Complete phase review
Evaluation	Release deliverable product to client
	Create user documentation
	Final phase/project review

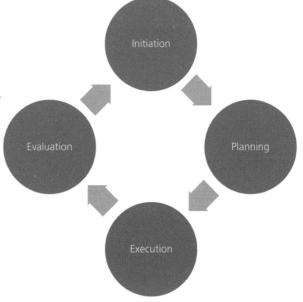

Figure 1.1 The project life cycle

A phase review occurs at the end of every stage. The review checks that all the tasks in a stage have been successfully completed so that the project can move to the next stage.

Initiation phase

The **resources** are the things that are needed to complete the project. These may include hardware and software and different specialist roles such as programmers and testers.

Constraints include:

- the timescale for the completion of the project
- the budget for the project
- security requirements, including legislation implications
- the hardware/software that should be used during the development of the final product
- the hardware/software that the final product should be compatible with.

The **feasibility report** defines the success criteria and objectives. The project manager will consult the client when these are being defined. Each of the questions and constraints is considered and a way forward is recommended – Go, No Go.

Figure 1.2 Defining the success criteria and objectives

Planning phase

The constraints and requirements that were defined in the feasibility report are used to create the project plans, and resource lists are created for the whole project (see Section 1.3, page 10).

Initial designs for the product are created. These could be screens for a user interface, a database structure or page plans.

The product will need to be tested during creation and after it has been completed. Initial test plans are created.

Resources The things needed to complete the project. These may include hardware and software and different specialist roles such as programmers and testers.

Feasibility report Created during the initiation stage and considers each of the questions and constraints. Success criteria and objectives are defined in this report. The report forms the basis on which the whole project should be completed.

Execution phase

The longest phase in the project life cycle.

The **project manager** will use the project plan(s) to monitor the project. The project must be kept on track so that the final product is delivered to the client on time – this is the time constraint.

The deliverable product is created and tested using the test plans that were created in the planning phase.

Evaluation phase

The deliverable product is released to the client. The product will have been thoroughly tested to make sure it works correctly and meets all the defined user requirements.

User documentation is created. This could include installation and user guides.

A final phase/project review is carried out, which focuses on:

- the success of the project against the defined success criteria and user requirements
- deviations from the original project plans and why these happened
- the processes and resources used and the effects of these on the project
- the **maintainability** of the product.

1.1.2 The advantages of following a project life cycle

REVISED

The advantages of following a project life cycle are that:

- it provides a structured approach
- it shows clearly defined tasks to be carried out in each phase
- the inputs and outputs of each phase are defined (see Section 1.3, page 10)
- the roles and responsibilities of each project team member are defined
- resources are allocated at the start of the project
- the project progress can be monitored to make sure the final product is delivered to the client on time.

Revision activity

Copy out Table 1.1, 'Tasks to be completed during each phase'. Cut up the table to separate the phases and the tasks. Mix them all up. Match each task with the correct phase.

Common mistake

The phases of the project life cycle must be followed in order. This is to make sure that all the tasks for each stage are fully completed before the next stage is started. Do not confuse the order of the phases or the tasks for each phase.

Exam tip

Make sure you know the advantages of following a project life cycle. You may need to select the most appropriate advantages for a scenario in your exam.

Project manager The person who is in overall charge of the project. They do not carry out any of the development tasks associated with the project but they manage the tasks, people and resources needed.

Maintainability Future development of the product in terms of the use of emerging technologies or adapting to any changes in the client's business or organisation.

Exam tip

Make sure you know the tasks that are completed in each phase of the project life cycle.

Now test yourself

1 Identify the second stage in the project life cycle.
   [1 mark]
2 Identify and describe **two** constraints that could be defined during the initiation phase.
   [6 marks]
3 Identify **two** different types of user documentation that could be created during the evaluation phase.
   [2 marks]
4 Describe **one** advantage of following a project life cycle that relates to the project team.   [2 marks]

TESTED

Now test yourself answers at www.hoddereducation.co.uk/myrevisionnotes

1.2 The interaction and iteration between the phases of the project life cycle

Each phase of the project life cycle interacts with the phase before it and after it.

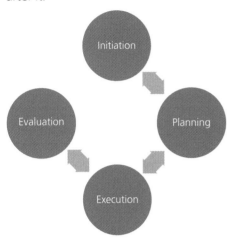

Figure 1.3 The interaction between the phases of the project life cycle

There is no interaction between the evaluation and initiation stages because when the evaluation phase has been completed, the project has been completed.

Table 1.2 The interaction and iteration between the phases

Phase	Interaction with:	Iteration with:
Initiation	Planning	
Planning	Initiation	Initiation
	Execution	
Execution	Planning	Planning
	Evaluation	
Evaluation	Execution	Execution

Each stage has defined outputs. These outputs are the inputs for the next phase of the project life cycle – the interaction (see Section 1.3, page 10).

Iterative reviews occur through the project life cycle at the end of each phase – these are phase reviews.

Iteration and interaction:

- occur between all the stages of the project life cycle, except between the evaluation and initiation stages
- can only occur between any given stage and the stage before or after it. The exception to this is the evaluation stage, as there is no stage after this.

If during the planning stage the project manager finds that not all the client's requirements have been defined, then the planning stage must stop and the project must return to the initiation stage.

Common mistake

Don't confuse iteration with interaction. Iteration is the repeating of a phase; interaction is how the phases link together.

Exam tip

Make sure you know the difference between iteration and interaction.

Iteration The repeating of a phase. Each repetition of a phase, when amendments are made, is called an iteration. The results of each iteration are used as the starting point for the next.

Interaction How the phases link together.

Remember

Each stage *must* be completed before moving to the next stage in the life cycle. If any of the tasks within a stage have *not* been successfully completed, then it is not possible to move on to the next stage. It is also possible that the project must return to the previous stage if any information is missing.

Revision activity

Copy out Table 1.2, 'The interaction and iteration between the phases'. Cut up the table to separate the phases. Mix them all up. Correctly match each phase with the one(s) it interacts and/or iterates with.

Now test yourself

1 Why is there no interaction between the evaluation and initiation stages? [3 marks]
2 Which phases interact with the execution phase? [2 marks]
3 Describe what is meant by 'interaction'. [3 marks]

TESTED

L01 Understand the tools and techniques that can be used to initiate and plan solutions

1.3 The inputs and outputs of each phase of the project life cycle

Part of the interaction between phases is the inputs and outputs for each phase. These are shown in Table 1.3.

Table 1.3 The inputs and outputs of each phase of the project life cycle

Phase	Inputs	Outputs
Initiation	User requirements User constraints	Feasibility report Legislation implications Phase review
Planning	Feasibility report Legislation implications	Project plan Test plan Constraints list Phase review
Execution	Project plan Test plan Constraints list	Deliverable product Test results Phase review
Evaluation	Deliverable product Test results	Release of deliverable product User documentation Final review report

Initiation phase inputs

User requirements:

● Define what the client wants the product to achieve.

● Are created between the client and the project manager.

● Can be general or specific.

User constraints:

● Are given to the project manager by the client.

● Are restrictions that must be adhered to during the creation of the product.

● Are comprised of four constraints – timescale, budget, hardware, software.

Initiation phase outputs, planning phase inputs

Feasibility report:

● Answers the questions asked during the initiation stage.

● Can also include different proposed solutions for the client.

● Considers the client-defined constraints and the requirements that have been set.

● Answers the question Go, No Go?

Legislation implications:

● Depend on the type of product being created and the **assets** being used.

● May need to be revisited during the project to check the legislation hasn't been updated.

Now test yourself answers at www.hoddereducation.co.uk/myrevisionnotes

Planning phase outputs, execution phase inputs

Project plan (see Section 1.5, page 17):

- Is created by the project manager.
- Forms the basis for completion of the project.
- Includes tasks, resources needed, **milestones**, **contingency time**, **workflow** and end date.

Test plan:

- During the planning phase, will be related to checking user requirements are being met.
- Could be produced, based on the type of product, to be used during the execution stage.

Constraints list:

- Created from the client-defined constraints provided in the initiation phase.
- Provides detailed information about each of the constraints.
- Is constantly referred to during the project life cycle.
- Referred to during the phase reviews to make sure that all the constraints are being met.

Execution phase outputs, evaluation phase inputs

Deliverable product:

- The product is created and tested.
- Bugs or errors found are corrected.
- Retests are carried out to ensure the product works as intended and meets the defined client or user requirements.

Test results:

- Tests are carried out both during creation and when completed.
- Test results will be recorded and checked to make sure that every part of the product has been tested.
- The results of any retests are recorded.

Evaluation phase outputs

Release of deliverable product:

- The product is fully checked against the constraints list and defined requirements.
- The product is installed on to the client's computer system.
- It is checked again to check it is working as intended.
- When the project team is happy, the product is released to the client.

User documentation:

- Created before the product is released to the client.
- The type of user documentation will depend on the type of product.

> **Assets** Items such as images or videos to be included in the final product.
>
> **Milestones** A given point in time when a task is expected to be started or completed.
>
> **Contingency time** Time in a project plan with no tasks assigned. This is used if tasks are not completed on time, to make sure the project still meets the final deadline.
>
> **Workflow** Which tasks are dependent on another, which tasks have to be completed before moving on to the next, and which tasks can be completed at the same time as others.

- Examples of user documentation:
  - A user guide showing how to use the product.
  - An installation guide, which could be used in the future if the product needs to be reinstalled.
  - Test plans showing the results of all testing carried out.
  - Security details, which show the built-in security and, for example, how to set up new users with access details.

At the end of each phase a phase review will be carried out. The tasks carried out will depend on the phase that has just been completed.

Table 1.4 The focus of the phase review for each phase of the project life cycle

Phase	Phase review tasks
Initiation	Consider the feasibility report
	Decide if the project is to carry on
	If omissions in information are found, the stage is repeated
Planning	Consider the project plan, test plans and the constraints list
	Check there are no omissions in the documents
	Either omissions and issues are resolved, or return to initiation phase (iteration)
	Project plan, test plans and constraints list checked and agreed by the client
Execution	Consider the completed product
	Review product against the test results, the user requirements and the constraints list
	Either omissions and issues are resolved, or phase repeated to resolve these
	Correct product signed off as fit for release to client
Evaluation	Consider all aspects of the project
	Measure success against criteria/objectives
	Review deviations from original plans
	Evaluate the effect of processes and resources on delivering solutions (software selected, tools and techniques used, compatibility of software and systems)
	Assess the maintainability of the product, including further development of system in future, use of emerging technologies, adapting to a changed environment

Revision activity

Copy out Table 1.3, 'The inputs and outputs of each phase of the project life cycle'. Cut up the table to separate the phases and the inputs and outputs. Mix them all up. Match each input and output with the correct phase.

Common mistake

It is important that you do not muddle the inputs and outputs for each phase of the project life cycle.

Now test yourself TESTED

1 Identify and describe **one** output from the initiation phase. [3 marks]
2 Identify **two** tasks that would be carried out during the planning phase review. [2 marks]

1.4 Initial project considerations

Objectives are set during the initiation phase. Objectives should be clearly defined and achievable, and help make sure the final product meets the needs of the client.

Initial project considerations will depend on the product being created. The main types are:

- SMART goals
- User requirements
- Success criteria
- Constraints/limitations – time, resources, regulations, security/risk management, mitigation of risks.

1.4.1 SMART goals

SMART stands for: **S**pecific, **M**easurable, **A**chievable, **R**ealistic, **T**ime.

- Specific: The client will provide a general idea of the type of product they want created. During the initiation phase, the project manager will discuss this with the client to get more details. The more details there are, the greater the chance of the final product meeting the needs of the client. This means that specific details and goals are defined. These details will also be used to monitor the project through the life cycle and to measure success or failure during the phase reviews.
- Measurable: Each goal that is set must be measurable. This enables the project manager to look at progress towards the goals during the project phase reviews (see Section 1.3, page 10).
- Achievable: The goals set must be achievable. If goals are set that are not achievable then this may cause the project to fail, with the deliverable product not meeting the client's requirements.
- Realistic: The goals set must be realistic in order that they can be achieved. A realistic goal is one that the project manager, and their team, can work towards and achieve.
- Time: Setting a realistic timescale is essential. This is set during the initiation phase and is used by the project manager to create the project plan (see Section 1.5, page 17). The timescale can be taken from the client's defined end date – when the product needs to be delivered by. This date will be used to work out how long the project will last and can be used when allocating the time for each task.

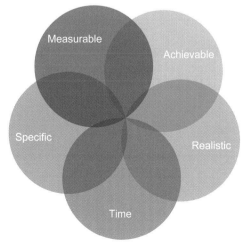

Figure 1.4 **How the SMART goals interact and interlink**

L01 Understand the tools and techniques that can be used to initiate and plan solutions

> **Exam tip**
>
> You may need to define SMART goals for a given scenario. Make sure you know what SMART stands for.

1.4.2 User requirements

REVISED

User requirements are defined and used during the initiation phase (see Section 1.3, page 10). They are referred to during each phase review to check they are still being met by the project. If it is found that the user requirements are not being met then changes can be made to the product.

1.4.3 Success criteria

REVISED

Success criteria are taken from what the client has said the product needs to do or include or its inputs/outputs.

Criteria need to be measurable, realistic and relevant. There is no point creating success criteria that are not measurable, relevant and/or realistic, as this will set the project up to fail!

Success criteria will be used in the phase reviews to help check the product is meeting the client's needs.

Time is one success criterion that *must* be defined. The client will define a date by which the product must be delivered. This also helps the project manager when creating the project plan (see Section 1.5, page 17).

Success criteria can be generic or specific. For example:

- Generic: 'Include original photographs.'
- Specific: 'Include photographs of sailing boats in a harbour.'

Other success criteria, depending on the product to be created, could include:

- the target audience
- the colours/font to be used
- the hardware platform the product is to be installed on
- the software that is to be used during the creation of the product and/or the user documentation
- how the product is to be accessed, for example through a network or via the cloud
- components to be used
- input and output format and contents.

> **Remember**
>
> If success criteria are not clearly defined then how can the success of the project be measured?

> **Remember**
>
> All success criteria, generic or specific, must be measurable, relevant and realistic.

1.4.4 Constraints/limitations

REVISED

Constraints/limitations include:

- time
- resources
- regulations
- security/risk management
- mitigation of risks.

Time and resources

Time and resources, such as budget, hardware and software, are usually defined by the client (see Section 1.1, page 6).

Now test yourself answers at www.hoddereducation.co.uk/myrevisionnotes

Regulations

Regulations and legislation must be considered during development of the product (see Section 4.5, page 62). These include:

- Health and Safety at Work Act (H&S)
- Data Protection Act (DPA)
- Computer Misuse Act (CMA)
- Copyright, Designs and Patents Act (CD&PA)
- Freedom of Information Act (FoI).

Which pieces of legislation or regulations need to be considered will depend on the type of product being created.

Table 1.5 Relevant legislation with examples of its application

Legislation/regulation	Example
Health and Safety at Work Act (H&S)	Product to be used in a noisy environment
Data Protection Act (DPA)	Personal data held about people
Computer Misuse Act (CMA)	Security of the product
Copyright, Designs and Patents Act (CD&PA)	Images to be used on a website
Freedom of Information Act (FoI)	Data and reports held about people/organisations

Security/risk management

Security management relates to logical and physical protection methods (see Section 4.4, page 57).

Logical protection methods include:

- firewalls
- encryption
- access rights
- usernames and passwords.

These protection methods can be used to conform to legislative requirements. They are created by the project team during the creation of the product as one of the tasks in the project plan.

Physical protection methods can include:

- Locking rooms that computer equipment is located in.
- Bolting computers to desks.
- Using device locks.
- Using and closing blinds at windows.

These are recommended by the project team but implemented by the client when the product has been released.

> **Exam tip**
>
> Make sure you know about, understand and can apply the most up-to-date version of each piece of legislation and regulation that is relevant to IT.

> **Logical protection methods** Computer-based methods that can be put in place by the development team or the network/systems administrator. These aim to reduce, or mitigate, the risks to data being stored.
>
> **Physical protection methods** Security methods that are designed to deny unauthorised access to computer equipment, resources or buildings.

[Handwritten notes:] Question on Logical protection: Computer-based methods put in place by network's administrator. They reduce the risks to data being stored. (and computer)

Physical: Security methods designed to deny unauthorised access to computer equipment etc.

Mitigation of risks

'Mitigation of risks' refers to the steps that can be taken to reduce the impact of setbacks or problems. Steps can include:

- Regular meetings with team to identify problems.
- Splitting complex tasks between development team members.
- Building in contingency time to project plans (see Section 1.5, page 17).

The most common risk is technical and relates to:

- hardware
- equipment
- software
- people.

Technical risk can be reduced by following procedures such as:

- File- and folder-naming conventions.
- Version control of the files and folders that are created and used.
- The processes for creating and storing backups of files and folders.

1.4.5 The purpose and importance of setting objectives

REVISED

- Objectives are set by the project manager and the client.
- They are the basis on which the project is based.
- The final deliverable product is measured against these.
- They are reviewed during phase reviews to make sure they are being met (see Section 1.3, page 10).
- If they are not being met, the project may have to return to the previous phase – iteration.

If correct objectives are set:

- The product will fully meet the defined client requirements.
- Nothing will be left out, so the product can be used as soon as it is ready.
- The product will be delivered in the agreed timescale.

> **Revision activity**
>
> Copy out Table 1.5, 'Relevant legislation with examples of its application'. Cut up the table to separate the legislation and the examples. Mix them all up. Correctly match each piece of legislation and example.

Now test yourself

TESTED

1 What does the M in SMART stand for? [1 mark]
2 Describe what is meant by the 'time constraint'. [4 marks]
3 Explain why it is important to set success criteria for a project. [4 marks]

> **Common mistake**
>
> Confusing the different pieces of legislation is a common mistake. Each piece of legislation has a different focus and can be applied to different scenarios.

1.5 Planning tools and the software types used to develop project plans

1.5.1 The purpose of planning tools

Some planning tools are used to create documentation to keep the project on track and monitor progress. They can be used during phase reviews (see Section 1.3, page 10) and can show:

- tasks/processes
- time allocated to each task
- task dependencies
- workflow
- milestones
- resources needed.

Some planning tools can be used to create initial designs for the final product.

Planning tools include:

- Gantt charts
- PERT (Project Evaluation and Review Technique) charts
- critical paths
- visualisation diagrams
- flow charts
- mind maps
- task lists.

These can be divided into formal and informal planning tools, as shown in Table 1.6.

Table 1.6 Formal and informal planning tools

Formal	Informal
Gantt chart	Flow chart
PERT chart	Mind map
Critical path	Task list
Visualisation diagram	

Gantt charts

A **Gantt chart** shows each task as a block of time, and shows:

- how long each task should take
- the order in which the tasks should be completed
- **concurrent** tasks
- **dependencies** between tasks
- milestones
- contingency time.

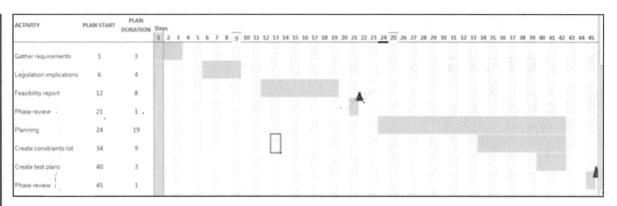

Figure 1.5 A Gantt chart

PERT charts

PERT stands for **P**roject **E**valuation and **R**eview **T**echnique. A PERT chart:

- uses circles or rectangles to represent tasks and milestones
- has lines between the tasks to show dependent tasks and time allocation
- represents concurrent tasks with two lines out of a task
- can be used to show the critical path.

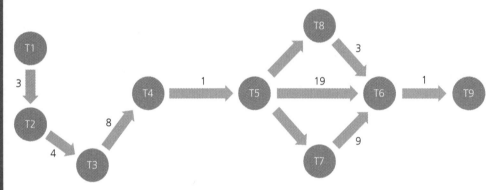

Figure 1.6 A PERT chart

Critical paths

- Show the longest path that the project should take to be completed.
- Show the shortest time that a project can be completed in, if all goes to plan.
- Are worked out by adding up the allocated time for all the dependent – not concurrent – tasks, including contingency time.
- Are used by the project manager to monitor the project to make sure every task is running to schedule.

Visualisation diagrams

- Are a rough drawing or sketch of what the final product will look like.
- Are used to visually plan the layout of a **static product**.
- Cannot be used for a product that has a timeline, such as a video.
- Can show the format and layout of outputs from a product such as a report.
- A graph is a visualisation diagram for numerical data.

Flow charts

- Are used to show the steps, decisions and outputs in a process.
- Can be used to create a simple diagram of all the steps that need to be carried out in a project.

Now test yourself answers at www.hoddereducation.co.uk/myrevisionnotes

- Set out each task in the proposed sequence – the order in which the tasks have to be completed.
- Give no indication of the timescale for each task.

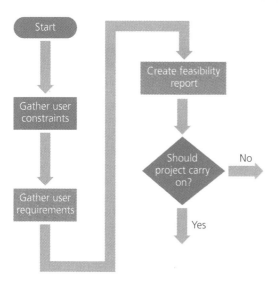

Figure 1.7 **A flow chart**

Mind maps

- Can also be called spider diagrams.
- Start with a target or goal, known as a central idea or node.
- Other tasks branch off the central node.
- Branches can have words on them.
- Branches are the lines that link the tasks or subtasks.

Task lists

- Show what tasks have to be completed, the start and end dates, and the **duration**.
- Include all the tasks that must be completed during a project.
- Some tasks may need breaking down into sub-tasks.
- Should be in a logical order; the tasks must flow from the initiation phase to the end of the evaluation phase.
- Can show the resources that will be needed for each task or sub-task.

Task	Start Date	End Date	Duration
Gather requirements	01-Mar	04-Mar	3
Legislation implications	06-Mar	10-Mar	4
Feasibility report	12-Mar	20-Mar	8
Phase review	21-Mar	22-Mar	1
Planning	24-Mar	12-Apr	19
Create constraints list	03-Apr	12-Apr	9
Create test plans	09-Apr	12-Apr	3
Phase review	14-Apr	15-Apr	1

Figure 1.8 **A task list**

Gantt chart A visual method of showing the proposed timing of each task needed to complete a project.

Concurrent Tasks that can be completed at the same time.

Dependency A dependent task is one that cannot be started until a previous, specified task has been completed.

Static product A product that doesn't move, for example a CD/DVD/Blu-ray cover, poster or magazine front cover.

Duration How much time a task should take to be completed.

1.5.2 Components of the planning tools

Each planning tool has components that can be linked. The tables below show the components for each planning tool.

Table 1.7 The components of the formal planning tools

Gantt chart	PERT chart	Visualisation diagram
Dates/days along the top	Nodes/sub-nodes	Multiple images/graphics
Tasks down the left side	Time/duration lines	Size and position of images/graphics
Blocks to represent the time allocated to each task	Task sequences	Position and style of text
Milestones as diamonds/triangles	Dependent tasks	Fonts
Dependent tasks	Concurrent tasks	Annotations
Concurrent tasks	Can show critical path	Colours/themes

Table 1.8 The components of the informal planning tools

Flow chart	Mind map	Task list
Start point	Nodes	Tasks
End point	Sub-nodes	Sub-tasks
Decisions	Branches/connecting lines	Start date
Processes	Key words	End date
Connecting lines	Colours	Duration
Direction arrows	Images	Resources

Exam tip

Make sure you know the different components for each type of planning tool.

1.5.3 The advantages and disadvantages of planning tools

Each planning tool has advantages and disadvantages, as shown in Table 1.9.

Table 1.9 The advantages and disadvantages of each planning tool

Planning tool	Advantages	Disadvantages
Gantt chart	Can show estimated time schedule Tasks are shown against a time schedule Comments can be added Resources for each task can be shown	Can be too simple for a complex project Task time is estimated so the plan may be unrealistic Task dependencies can be difficult to identify at the start of a project Not easy to identify the critical path
PERT and critical path	Can show slack time so resources can be reallocated Enables timescales to be planned Tasks can be scheduled as dependent or concurrent	Can become confusing Needs skill and knowledge to create Can be limited in large and complex projects

Planning tool	Advantages	Disadvantages
Visualisation diagram	Information and data can be quickly understood Emerging trends and patterns can be quickly spotted Non-specialists can understand the data/numbers being shown	Not appropriate for large and complex projects
Flow chart	Can be useful for simple projects with a small number of tasks and decisions No specialist project-planning knowledge needed to understand the flow chart	Does not show time allocated for each task Tasks shown sequentially so does not show concurrent tasks
Mind map	Easy to add ideas/tasks at any time Can provide focus on the tasks and the links between them Shows dependent tasks	No time schedule Can be difficult for others to understand Does not show concurrent tasks
Task list	Can provide focus on the tasks to be completed No tasks will be missed out	Should not be used for large or complex projects

Remember

The choice of project-planning tool will depend on the project being completed. In some cases, if a planning tool is used that is not appropriate or useful this is worse than having no plan at all!!

1.5.4 Software types used

REVISED

Different software can be used to create planning documentation. The software that could be used includes:

- project management software
- spreadsheets
- word processors
- DTP (desktop publishing).

Project management software

Project management software can be used to create Gantt and PERT charts, including defining the critical path. The tools required, for example to link tasks or define milestones, are built into the software.

L01 Understand the tools and techniques that can be used to initiate and plan solutions

Table 1.10 The strengths and weaknesses of project management software

Strengths	Weaknesses
Real-time changes can be made	Some project-planning software is very expensive
Project plans can be shared electronically	There is a possibility that a simple project can become very complicated
Project plans can include allocated resources	Can be time-consuming to set up a project
Reports can be generated, for example to show the resources needed to complete each task	May need some knowledge, training or experience to use the software

Spreadsheets

- Are designed to store and manipulate numbers, using functions and formulas.
- May include a template for a simple Gantt chart.
- Do not allow comments or audit trails to be created or seen by all members of the project team.
- Are not designed to store files, annotations or any communication or collaboration, which are essential to make a project successful.
- Can be used to create a task list, where a formula can total the number of days allocated for each task or the total number of days.

Word processors

- Can be used to create a range of plans, including a task list or mind map.
- Include in-built tools and features that allow shapes and lines to be used to create flow charts.

Desktop publishing

- Can be used to create a visualisation diagram, a mind map or a spider diagram.
- Can combine and import components from different files, for example a scanner, graphics package or a word-processing file.
- Can **group** components.

> **Exam tip**
>
> You may need to select and describe a planning tool based on a scenario. You will need to select the most appropriate planning tool software based on the type of plan to be created. Make sure you know the advantages and disadvantages of each type of software.

> **Group/grouping** Several components can be moved as one. A feature usually found in DTP or word-processing software.

> **Revision activity**
>
> Copy out Table 1.9, 'The advantages and disadvantages of each planning tool'. Cut up the table to separate the tools and the advantages and disadvantages. Mix them all up. Match each advantage and disadvantage with the correct planning tool.

> **Common mistake**
>
> Selecting an inappropriate planning tool is a common mistake. Each planning tool has a different purpose and is best for creating particular types of plans.

Now test yourself

TESTED ☐

1. Describe the purpose of a visualisation diagram. [3 marks]
2. Identify **two** components of a Gantt chart. [2 marks]
3. Describe **one** advantage and **one** disadvantage of using a mind map as a planning tool. [4 marks]

LO3 Understand how data and information can be collected, stored and used

3.1 Data

3.1.1 What data is

REVISED

Data is **raw facts and figures before they have been processed**.
The main points about data are:

- Data has no meaning.
- Data is raw facts and figures before they have been processed.
- Data can be made up of letters, numbers, symbols, graphics and sound.

3.1.2 Data types and how they are used

REVISED

Data needs to be stored before it can be processed. A **data type** needs to be chosen – this is based on the characteristics of data being stored and how it is to be processed.

The main data types are shown in Table 3.1.

Table 3.1 The different data types and how they could be used

Data type	Description	Example of data	How it could be used
Text	Any character	DB7&~?>hT5	To store names of items or people. Phone numbers are usually stored as text as this means they can have spaces and start with a 0
Alphanumeric	Any combination of letters, symbols, spaces or numbers	AjcY6&9£4	To store postcodes, as these contain numbers and letters
Integer number	Whole numbers	1960	To store number of items in stock, number of lengths swum, number of tickets sold in one day to a live concert, TV channel number, years
Real number	Any number, with or without decimal places	12.30	To store height/weight
Currency	Shows data in a format of money. It can be used to show currency signs (e.g. £ or $) and have decimal places to show the full currency details	£79.87	To store prices
Percentage	A number format that includes decimal places and a % sign	25%	To show a percentage of a discount, e.g. 25% off the price

Data type	Description	Example of data	How it could be used
Fraction	A number format, usually included in spreadsheet software, that enables actual fractions to be input and manipulated	$\frac{7}{8}$	To show the result of a calculation
Decimal	A number format that shows an exact number using a decimal point and numbers after the decimal point	22.75	To show the result of a calculation expressed as a decimal
Date/time	A date or time – there are different formats of date and time that can be used. Which one is chosen will depend on how the date/time is to be stored and processed	25/04/2017 19:15	To show a date, e.g. 25 April 2017, or a time, e.g. 19:15 or 7:15 p.m.
Limited choice	Restricts a user's choice; can be used on an information-gathering document	A drop-down list, radio button, tick list	To select a day of the week, or a radio button to select a payment method
Object	An additional component, usually found in a spreadsheet	A chart or graph taken from a different source	To insert a chart into a worksheet that has been taken from a different file
Logical/Boolean	There are only two choices, e.g. true or false	Yes or no, true or false, male or female, 1 or 0	To store the gender of a person, or to answer a closed question

Revision activity

Copy out Table 3.1, 'The different data types and how they could be used'. Cut up the table to separate the data types, descriptions, examples of data and how they could be used. Mix them all up. Match each data type with the correct description, example of data and how it could be used.

Exam tip

Make sure you know the different data types and what data can be stored using each one. You may need to select the most appropriate data type for data given to you in your exam.

Data types A specific kind of data item that is defined by the values that can be stored using it or how the data is going to be processed.

3.2 Information

3.2.1 What information is

Information is created when data is processed. The formula for converting data to information is:

> **Information = data + [structure] + [context] + meaning**

> **Information** Processed data that has a meaning and is in context.

The structure of data is how it is presented. For example:

Data type	Structure	Example
Date	NN/NN/NNNN	24/04/2017
Alphanumeric	LLNN NLL	Postcode

Context is the environment that we know and understand to make sense of the data. For example:

Data	15, cabbages, rabbits
Context	15 cabbage plants were planted but the rabbits ate all of them

The meaning of data is revealed when it is in the correct structure and put into context. For example:

Data	Structure	Context	Meaning
01012017	NN/NN/NNNN	A UK date	New Year's Day in 2017
30 40 50 60 70	Integer numbers	Miles per hour	Speed limits on different types of UK roads and motorways
TRNB14	First two letters: type of clothing Second two letters: colour Last two numbers: UK women's clothes size LLLLNN	A clothing shop stock code	A navy-blue pair of trousers, UK size 14

3.2.2 How data and information are related

You have already learned about how information is:

> **data + [structure] + [context] + meaning**

Data and information are related. This means that there are links between data and information. The main links you need to be aware of are that:

- Information is in context, while data has no context.
- Information is data that has been coded/structured.
- Data must be processed to become information.

Common mistake

When you are selecting a data type for a piece of data, make sure that the data type you select is appropriate. For example, most people think that a telephone number is stored as a numerical data type. This is wrong because a telephone number starts with a 0 so the data type will be text.

Revision activity

Fill in the table below to show how data can be turned into information. The first one has been done for you.

	Shoe shop	Library	Football team
Data	MTNSS10		
Structure	LLLLLNN		
Context	A shoe shop stock code		
Meaning	Men's trainers, non-slip soles, size 10		

Now test yourself

TESTED ☐

1 For each of the examples, select an appropriate data type for storing it in a database:
   a 28 March 1969   [1 mark]
   b CB21 7WX   [1 mark]
   c Girl or Boy   [1 mark]
   d The name of your centre   [1 mark]
   e 567   [1 mark]
2 Give **one** reason why a telephone number would be stored as the text data type.   [2 marks]
3 Describe **one** difference between information and data.   [2 marks]

3.3 The methods used to collect data and store data/information, and the IT used to support data collection

3.3.1 The methods used to collect and store data/information

REVISED

Methods to collect and store data/information

The method that is chosen to collect data and information will depend on:

- What data and information is to be collected.
- Where the data and information is to be collected.
- How the collected data and information will be stored and processed.

Questionnaires/surveys

Questionnaires and surveys contain a set of questions that are used to collect data and information. The questions can be:

- **closed**
- **open**
- **rank order**
- **rating**.

The questionnaire/survey can be completed either online or on hard copy (paper).

Online questionnaires/surveys can be provided by email, on a website or on the cloud. As each person completes and submits their answers, the data and information can be automatically input into the software being used for the analysis. This method means there is less chance of errors in the data/information being stored and processed.

> **Closed question** A question with only a set number of answers to be chosen from, for example for 'Can you ride a bicycle?' the answers would be either 'Yes' or 'No'.
>
> **Open question** Allows the person completing the questionnaire to give a detailed answer in their own words.
>
> **Rank order** Requires the person completing the questionnaire to rank a list of items in order, for example from 1 to 10 where 1 is the most important and 10 is the least important.
>
> **Rating** Requires the person completing the questionnaire to rate items on a list individually, for example from 1 to 10 where 1 is very important and 10 is least important.

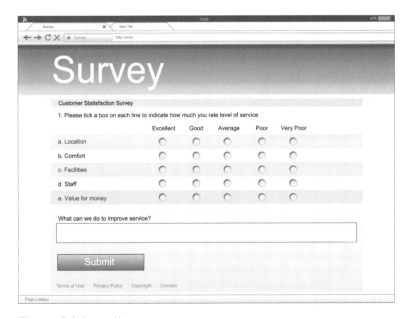

Figure 3.1 An online survey

Alternatively, a questionnaire can be completed on paper and collected when complete. The data and information must then be manually input into the software package before any processing can be carried out. This can often introduce errors.

Email

Emails can be sent that include:

- An interactive form to be completed and returned to the sender. The collected data and information can be automatically imported into a spreadsheet or database as long as the form contains the same fields in the same order.
- A link to an online survey, where the process is the same as that for a questionnaire.

Sensors

A sensor is a device that responds to a change or input from the environment.

- Inputs can include light, heat or motion.
- The output is usually a signal that is converted to a human-readable display or transmitted electronically over a network for reading or further processing.

There are many different types of sensors. One type is Passive Infrared (PIR) motion sensors, which work by detecting heat, for example when someone walks past the PIR. Examples of use of PIR sensors include switching an outside light on and off, or activating a burglar alarm. They can be part of a connected house.

Figure 3.2 A motion sensor in an outside light

PIR sensors can also be used to count. Data is collected each time the infrared beam is broken. Where the beam is located must be considered, however, as the wrong location can lead to false data being collected.

Pressure sensors are activated and count the pressure going across the pressure mat. The location must be carefully considered, as for PIR sensors. The data is automatically collected and stored. Examples of use include counting cars going along a road, or counting the number of people entering or leaving a building.

Interviews

An interview is a conversation between two people where questions are asked, usually one to one, face to face. The **interviewer** asks pre-planned questions of the **interviewee**. The questions asked will depend on the data and information that is to be collected and how it will be stored and processed. The data and information gathered during the interview will need to be manually input into the software being used to store and process it.

Consumer panels

A consumer panel is a group of people who give feedback through a series of questions. Examples include feedback on a new product/service (for instance a website or advert) or an initial design/mock-up of a new product. The panel is usually a cross-section of different ages, jobs, etc., to get a range of feedback and opinions. The feedback is collected face to face or via an online questionnaire.

Loyalty schemes

A loyalty scheme is a points-based rewards programme offered by a business to its customers. Members earn points each time they use the business. Points can be changed into rewards such as money-off vouchers for shopping, goods, days out to a tourist attraction or free hotel stays.

Figure 3.3 Loyalty scheme cards

The data collected can target offers to a customer based on their shopping history.

Statistical reports

Statistics can be found on websites, but the validity of the website *must* be checked. Trusted websites include those of the Office for National Statistics (ONS) and government departments. The statistics can be analysed to gather further data and information. Trends and patterns can be spotted.

Secondary research methods

There are two types of research methods – **primary** and **secondary**, as shown in Table 3.2.

Table 3.2 The characteristics of primary and secondary research

Characteristic	Primary research	Secondary research
Meaning	Research that collects first-hand or fresh data for a specific purpose	Research that uses data and information that has already been collected
Based on	Raw data and information	Analysed and processed data and information
Carried out by	The researcher	Someone else
Data	Specific to the purpose	May not fully meet the specific needs
Process	Very involved	Quick and easy
Cost	High	Low
Time	Long	Short

Research methods can be categorised as primary and secondary as shown in Table 3.3.

Table 3.3 Classification of methods of collecting data

Primary	Secondary
Questionnaires	Statistical and trends/reports
Sensors	Loyalty schemes
Interviews	
Loyalty schemes	

Exam tip

In your exam you may need to select and justify a collection method for a given context. Make sure that the collection method is appropriate for the type of information and data being collected.

Revision activity

Copy out Table 3.2, 'The characteristics of primary and secondary research'. Cut up the table to separate the characteristics for each type of research. Mix them all up. Match each characteristic to the correct research method.

Common mistake

Make sure that you know the differences between primary and secondary research methods. It is very easy to confuse the two methods.

Now test yourself

TESTED ☐

1 Compare the use of online and paper-based surveys. [4 marks]
2 Describe **two** differences between primary and secondary research. [4 marks]
3 Identify and describe **one** type of sensor. [3 marks]

Interviewer The person asking the questions.

Interviewee The person answering the questions.

Primary research method When the data and information collected is fresh data collected for a specific purpose.

Secondary research methods Methods that use data and information that has already been collected, for example using a book or website to find out statistics that have already been collected and, possibly, processed.

Appropriateness of data collection methods

Each method of collecting data and information has advantages and disadvantages. These are shown in Table 3.4.

Table 3.4 The advantages and disadvantages of different methods of collecting data and information

Method	Advantages	Disadvantages
Questionnaires/ surveys	Large numbers of people can be asked to fill in the same questionnaire/survey Comparisons are easy to formulate (e.g. 75 per cent of people liked the new company logo) Cheaper than interviews for large numbers of people	If the questionnaire/survey is online, people need the technology to be able to complete it A badly designed question may not get the data required in the right format
Emails	The same email can be sent to many people at the same time The results from the emails can be automatically input into software for analysis/manipulation Little risk of human error occurring when the data collected is input into the software	Emails may be diverted into spam/junk folders by the email provider If the fields or data types are not exactly the same as the fields being used for analysis/manipulation, the data collected may be worthless
Sensors	Once set up, do not need human intervention as the data collected can be sent electronically The data collected by a sensor is usually more accurate than that taken by people, for example people may lose count but sensors just keep working	The positioning of sensors needs to be carefully considered as incorrect placing could result in worthless data being collected Sensors may stop working, for example if there is a power cut
Interviews	Questions can be modified based on the answers given to previous questions A rapport can develop between the interviewer and the interviewee that may result in questions being answered honestly Additional questions can be asked to clarify any answers already given	Can be time-consuming and costly to carry out Poor interviewing can lead to misleading or insufficient data and information being gathered Not suitable for gathering data and information from large numbers of people
Consumer panels	The cost of consumer-panel feedback can be low if online feedback methods are used The feedback provided is specific to the product or service Response rates are high as members of the panel have agreed to take part	If products need to be provided to the panel, the cost may be high in terms of the actual product and the delivery to members of the panel If there isn't a range of people on the panel, the feedback could be biased towards one specific type of person The format of the feedback needs to match the processing that is to be carried out

Method	Advantages	Disadvantages
Loyalty schemes	A loyalty scheme can help keep customers using the business The data collected each time a customer uses their loyalty card can provide information on the habits of the customer	Some people feel that the data collected about them by using a loyalty scheme can be an invasion of privacy
Statistical reports	If a trusted source is used, then the statistics are readily available, cover a range of topics and are reliable Some processing may have already been carried out Statistics can show trends and patterns that can help with decision making	May not have been collected for the same purpose so may not provide clear and full data Statistics need to be collected knowing how they are going to be analysed/processed and stored Statistics show data from a sample of people rather than a true representation
Secondary research methods	The data has already been collected and possibly processed Data collection is quicker than having to collect the data first-hand	The data may not be exactly what is required It is not always possible to tell if the data is real/genuine

Revision activity

Copy out Table 3.4, 'The advantages and disadvantages of different methods of collecting data and information'. Cut up the table to separate the advantages and disadvantages of each collection method. Mix them all up. Match the advantages and disadvantages to the correct collection method.

Exam tip

In your exam you may need to provide the advantages and disadvantages of a collection method in a given context. Make sure that the advantages and disadvantages you give are appropriate for and relate to the context.

Now test yourself

TESTED ☐

1 Describe **two** advantages of using a consumer panel when collecting information about a new product. [4 marks]
2 Describe **one** advantage and **one** disadvantage of using a paper questionnaire to collect information. [4 marks]

3.3.2 Information technology used to support data collection

IT can be used to support data collection in the following ways.

Barcode readers

- Barcode readers are used to scan barcodes.
- Every product has a unique identifiable barcode.
- The barcode stores data about the product.
- Barcodes can help retailers identify products and use the information for stock control.

Uses include:

- Loyalty schemes: Products bought by a shopper are scanned and linked to the shopper's unique loyalty scheme number. The supermarket can identify which goods the shopper buys and use this information to target offers, discounts and money-off vouchers.
- Scan and shop: Members of a loyalty scheme can scan their own products. The data about their shopping is transferred to a checkout and linked to their loyalty scheme number.
- Stock control: When products are sold the barcode is used to remove the quantity bought from the stock database. When new products are delivered, the quantity is added to the stock database using the barcode.

Quick Response (QR) codes

- QR codes are two-dimensional barcodes that store data.
- They are made up of black modules arranged in a square pattern on a white background.
- They can hold more data and be read faster than a standard barcode.

Uses include:

- Advertising: QR codes are found in magazines, for example. The codes can be read, or scanned, by a smartphone using an app. The information held in the QR code – for example a URL, a discount voucher or the contact details of a business – can then be interpreted by the smartphone.

Web-based surveys

- Web-based surveys are surveys that are located on the internet.
- They can be sent as a link or URL contained in an email.
- To access and complete them, a device – such as a smartphone, tablet or computer connected to the internet – must be used.
- When the survey has been completed, the responses are submitted.
- The submitted responses are automatically saved and stored, usually in a spreadsheet or database.

Uses include:

- Voting for a talent show on TV.
- Surveys from manufacturers about products purchased.
- Feedback after a holiday or hotel stay.

ISBN 978-1-5104-2327-5

Figure 3.4a A barcode

Figure 3.4b A barcode reader

Figure 3.5 A QR code

LO3 Understand how data and information can be collected, stored and used

There are IT methods   If asked for Data collection methods, use: Loyalty schemes, Statistical reports etc.

Wearable technology

- 'Wearable technology' refers to smart electronic devices that can be worn.
- It includes activity trackers, smart watches and headsets.
- It is a good example of the **Internet of Things**.

Data is sent on a file to manufacturer (company)'s database. Trends and patterns in fitness can help activity etc.

Uses include:

- An activity tracker that stores the wearer's fitness data in a file on the manufacturer's website. Progress can be tracked and compared with that of friends.
- Glasses that can deliver text notifications via a heads-up display in the glasses. Apps can be used by the glasses, for example to read out newspaper articles.

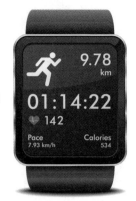

Figure 3.6 Wearable technology

Mobile technologies

- Mobile technology is any device that can be transported by the user.
- Mobile devices provide the user with instant access to information via the internet.

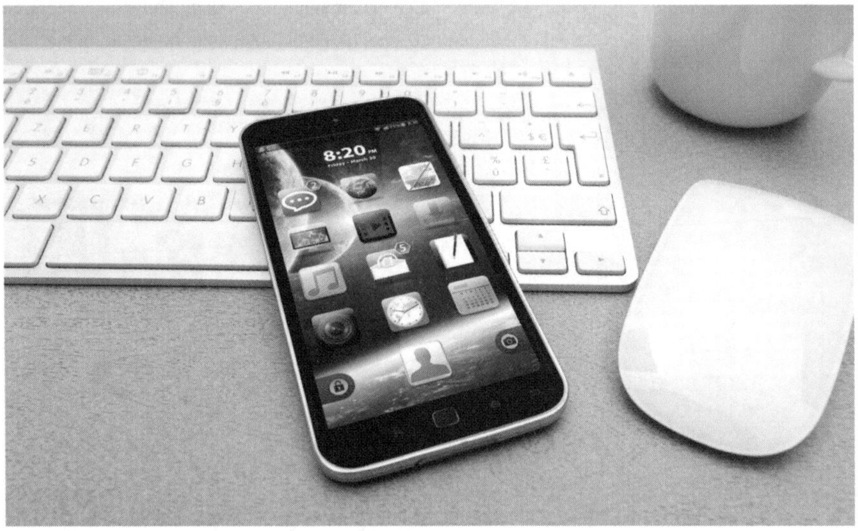

Figure 3.7 Mobile technology

> **Exam tip**
>
> You will need to keep up to date with developments and emerging technologies during your course. You may be expected to demonstrate this up-to-date knowledge in your exam.

Uses include:

- Smartphones, tablets, GPS devices such as satnavs, and e-book readers.
- Files and documents can be accessed 'on the move' through the cloud.

> **Internet of Things** The interconnection via the internet of computing devices embedded in everyday objects, enabling them to send and receive data.

Now test yourself

TESTED

1. Describe **one** advantage and **one** disadvantage of using mobile technology to access files and documents via the cloud. [4 marks]
2. Describe **one** use of barcode readers in a supermarket. [4 marks]

(3.4) Different storage methods and the appropriateness of the use of these in context

When data and information has been collected, it needs to be stored before it can be processed.

You will need to know about the cloud and physical devices.

3.4.1 The cloud

'The cloud' refers to software, services and storage areas that run on the internet rather than being stored and accessed on a physical storage device.

- It has a very large storage capacity.
- It is made up of a lot of servers that store and locate data and information.
- It is accessed through a web browser, such as Mozilla Firefox or Google Chrome, or through an app.

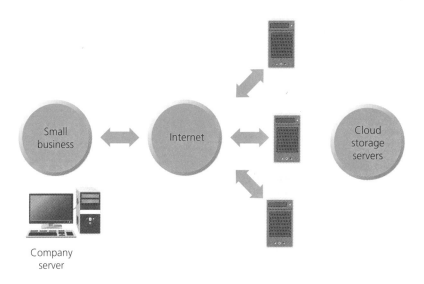

Figure 3.8 How the cloud stores files

Cloud services include Dropbox, Microsoft OneDrive and Amazon Drive. Files can be stored and accessed from anywhere via a device connected to the internet. This means that less physical storage is needed.

- Data can be processed as well as stored on the cloud.
- People can work remotely but still collaborate through files stored on the cloud.

Problems of using the cloud include:

- An internet connection is required to access and work on files. Without this, files, software and apps stored on the cloud can be inaccessible.
- If the cloud servers stop working ('go down'), the files, software and apps are inaccessible.
- The cloud storage area could be hacked, meaning information can get into the wrong hands. Security measures must be implemented (see Section 4.4, page 57).

LO3 Understand how data and information can be collected, stored and used

Table 3.5 The most common physical devices

Storage device	Features	Typical uses
Hard disk drive using magnetic disks	A hard disk drive uses magnetic disks for storing software and data in files The disks are circular and spin at high speeds while drive heads read and write the data; this makes the disks susceptible to dirt and damage if moved suddenly The files can be read, edited, re-written or deleted Hard disks can store huge amounts of data	Storage of the operating system Storage of files and data not currently in use Storage of data, files and software when the computer is turned off Storage of a database of the details of members
Solid state drive	A solid state drive uses flash memory to store software and data in files There are no moving parts in solid state drives, which makes them faster and more reliable than magnetic hard disk drives They are often found in portable computers such as netbooks and tablet computers Solid state drives are faster in use than hard disks They can store as much data as a hard drive, but are much more expensive to buy	Storage of the operating system Storage of files and data not currently in use Storage of data, files and software when the computer is turned off
Optical device	An optical drive uses optical media, such as CDs and DVDs, to store software and data in files The files can be read, edited, re-written or deleted only if CD-R/RWs or DVD-R/RWs are used Data stored on CD-ROMs and DVD-ROMs can be read but cannot be altered Blu-ray disks are optical disks and can store very large amounts of data	Storage of files or data that have to be moved to another computer Storage software for installation on a computer Storage of data, files and software in backups or archives

Storage device	Features	Typical uses
Flash memory devices	Small memory sticks contain flash memory and are used in USB ports They are used to store data and files for transfer to other computers, for taking to/from the office, in cameras and phones as the memory card	To save a file on to a memory stick (flash memory device) To save images in a camera To save contact details in a phone

Exam tip

In your exam, you may need to be able to select and justify the storage devices to be used in a context. Make sure that the storage device you select is the most appropriate one.

Revision activity

Copy out Table 3.5, 'The most common physical devices'. Cut up the table to separate the storage devices, features and typical uses. Mix them all up. Correctly match each device, feature and typical use.

Now test yourself

TESTED ☐

1 Describe **one** advantage and **one** disadvantage of employees who work remotely accessing files stored on the cloud. [4 marks]
2 Compare the use of CDs and DVDs to store files. [4 marks]
3 Identify **two** uses of a USB memory stick. [2 marks]

L03 Understand how data and information can be collected, stored and used

3.5 The use of data, the applications and interaction of data stores, and the benefits and drawbacks of the use of data

3.5.1 Big Data

REVISED ☐

Big Data is data sets that are so big or complex that traditional data-processing software cannot deal with them. Big Data is usually measured in terms of petabytes (1024 terabytes) or exabytes (1024 petabytes).

Big Data really is big!!

Big Data is about how data is collected, processed and stored. Trends and patterns can be found by analysing Big Data.

Little data stores can interact with Big Data stores. Big Data stores can also interact to form even bigger data stores.

3.5.2 Applications and interaction of data stores

REVISED ☐

Law enforcement

ANPR checks the number plate of every vehicle it sees and interacts with the DVLA to check:

- who is the owner of the vehicle
- if they have a current driving licence
- if the car is taxed and insured
- if the vehicle has a current MOT.

> **ANPR** Automatic Number Plate Recognition.

If there is a problem with the vehicle then an alert is displayed on the screen of the ANPR device in the police car.

Speed cameras are found on roads and motorways.

- The camera takes a measurement of the speed of a vehicle.
- If the vehicle is travelling at, or below, the speed limit then no action is taken.
- If the speed limit is being broken, then the camera takes a picture of the number plate.
- The number plate is looked up using the DVLA database.
- A speeding notice is sent to the registered owner of the vehicle.

Figure 3.9 A speed camera

CCTV cameras are used to monitor what is happening in a street, shopping centre, railway station or airport.

- A video screen is linked to the CCTV camera.
- Any suspicious activity spotted is passed to the emergency services who will deal with the problem.
- CCTV cameras can link to facial-recognition systems held by the police and other security services.
- Facial-recognition systems allow the security services to track people they feel are suspicious or whom they want to arrest.

The Police National Database enables all police forces in the UK to share information about criminal activity.

Figure 3.10 CCTV monitoring

Education

Schools can use data to analyse how well students are doing and how much progress they are making.

- Many colleges and universities offer **MOOCs**.
- The data and information entered by students as they are completing the course is collected.
- This is processed and analysed to provide students with a grade when they have completed the course.
- Changes to the courses can be made based on the data and information collected.
- Schools in different parts of the world can use the data that has been collected, stored and processed to help with their students' studies.
- Data that is stored and accessed through the cloud can be accessed and downloaded when it is not possible to use primary sources to collect the required data.

Health and fitness

Wearable technology was covered in Section 3.3.2 (page 34).

Research teams based worldwide conducting research into disease and illnesses share data. The collected, stored and processed data can be shared, usually through the cloud – an example of Big Data.

Apps can be used to collect data. People with a specific medical condition can input their own readings, for example blood glucose levels for people with diabetes. This data can be collected from a wider range of people and more quickly than if the research team had to collect it themselves.

Shopping

Retailers capture information and data every time a shopper uses their loyalty card. Loyalty schemes were covered in Section 3.3.1 (page 29).

The collected data is stored and processed to identify trends and patterns in shopping habits or to identify which products should be on special offer.

Data can be collected at the checkouts or from online shopping baskets. This provides details of every product sold. Manufacturers can use this data to target marketing, advertising and special offers.

Entertainment/leisure

Big Data is collected when a digital or satellite TV channel is watched, a film or music is streamed, and when people go to the cinema. Film and TV producers can also see how popular **box sets** have been. Films and TV programmes are made based on the data collected.

Satellite TV companies can use the data to suggest programmes a viewer may like to watch based on their previous viewing patterns. Music-streaming websites also suggest tracks and artists based on an individual's past music download choices.

The data can be analysed to predict what type of programmes, films and music people want to watch or listen to. This is done by looking at viewing history, searches, reviews and ratings, and at the device the content is watched or listened to on.

> **MOOC** A Massive Open Online Course is an online course with unlimited numbers of students and with open access via a website.
>
> **Box set** A complete set of programmes in a series, which can be downloaded and watched one after the other.

The analysed data can help advertisers provide advertising based on, for example, the age group of the people who are watching.

Lifestyle

Lifestyle applications include:

- cars that can automatically call for help
- solar panels on house roofs feeding power back into the National Grid
- connected houses.

Social media also collects, processes and analyses data and information from users.

SOS buttons

When an SOS button in a car is pressed, a signal is sent to the manufacturer's assistance team. When the signal is received, the position of the car is also provided so that help and assistance can be sent. The registration number of the car will be located and, if up-to-date contact details are available, the owner of the car can be contacted.

Figure 3.11 An SOS button

A tracking system can be activated if the car is stolen. A signal is sent to the tracking system assistance team and the police showing the location of the car and, if it is being driven, the route being taken. This sharing of data can help recover stolen cars.

Solar panels

Data can be collected about **green energy**, including solar panels.

Figure 3.12 Solar panels on a house roof

Electricity is generated for the household when the sun shines on the panels. If too much energy is produced, the spare electricity is fed back into the National Grid to add to the electricity supply.

Data is collected and can be analysed to see where the best locations are for solar panels, how much energy is generated by the solar panels and what percentage of the electricity needs of the UK is met by the generation of electricity by solar panels.

Connected houses

Connected houses supply and use data.

Smart meters send readings every few seconds of how much gas and electricity is being used. This data provides accurate bills to the customer and can be analysed by the suppliers to see, for example, at what time of day and night the most or least gas and electricity is being used. Suppliers can use this data to forecast how much gas and electricity they will need to supply in future months.

Door locks can report to the owner of the house and the security company if there is any unauthorised movement into or out of the house. This data could be used by insurance companies to find out which areas are the least and most likely to be burgled and to set the prices for house insurance accordingly.

Social media

Social media is a significant source of Big Data. Data is collected every time:

- someone likes or dislikes a page, video or photograph
- a page, photograph or video is shared, followed, retweeted or commented on.

The data can help marketing companies target products. For example, they could use it to find out which age group and gender would best be targeted with a discount on the price of a gym membership.

> **Revision activity**
>
> For each of the applications of data, find out one more use.

Green energy The use of natural, renewable resources to generate power.

GIGO Garbage In, Garbage Out.

3.5.3 The benefits and drawbacks of the use of data

Some of the benefits of using data include:

- Large amounts of data can be found using a range of data stores.
- Searches can be made to find the specific data required.
- Time does not need to be spent collecting new data.
- Data can be shared by teams carrying out the same tasks.
- A range of different analyses can be carried out on data.
- Data stores can interact to share data, for example the police and DVLA.

Some of the drawbacks to the use of data include:

- It is not always possible to know that the data is correct if it has been gathered by someone else.
- Errors in the data can have negative impacts on people.
- It may not be possible to get the specific data required.
- Data must be kept up to date, with the data owners being informed when updates are made.
- Incorrect data can lead to incorrect results – **GIGO.**
- Sensitive data must be securely stored with good data-security measures.

Exam tip

Make sure you know about each of the applications and how it uses data. You must know about the benefits and drawbacks of the use of data and be able to apply this knowledge to the different application areas.

Now test yourself

1 Identify and describe **two** ways in which data could be used in a connected house. [6 marks]
2 Explain how the data produced by viewing figures for a TV programme could be used when new TV shows are being created. [4 marks]
3 Discuss the advantages and drawbacks of the use of data in law enforcement. [8 marks]

LO3 Understand how data and information can be collected, stored and used

LO4 Understand the factors to be considered when collecting and processing data and storing data/information

4.1 Types of threats

There are many different threats to data and information. Some threats can also be targeted at physical computer equipment.

4.1.1 Botnet

REVISED

A **botnet** is usually the result of several computers being infected by a bot malware. This then allows the botnet, and the person who created it, to take control of the computer systems.

4.1.2 Malware

REVISED

Malware (malicious software) is installed on a computer system and collects information about users without their knowledge.

Table 4.1 The types of malware

Type of malware	Why it is used	How it works	How to mitigate its effects
Adware	**Adware** generates revenue for its author	Automatically shows adverts, such as pop-ups. It may also be in the user interface of a software package or on an installation screen. Adware, by itself, is harmless; however, some adware may include spyware such as key loggers	Install, run and keep updated a security software package Do not open any files from an unknown source Do not click any links in emails
Bot	Bots take control of a computer system	Allows a cyber-security attacker to take control of an infected computer system without the user's knowledge	Install, run and keep updated a security software package Do not open any files from an unknown source Do not click any links in emails

Type of malware	Why it is used	How it works	How to mitigate its effects
Bug	Bugs are connected to software and are flaws that produce unwanted outcomes	Usually the result of human error during the coding of the software. Most bugs can be fixed by the software creator issuing a fix or patch. Security bugs are the most severe type and can allow cyber attackers to bypass user authentication, override access privileges or steal data	Check for and install any patches that are released from software vendors
Ransomware	Ransomware holds a computer system captive and demands a ransom, usually money, to release it	Restricts user access to the computer system by encrypting files or locking down the computer system. A message is usually displayed to force the user to pay so that the restrictions can be lifted and the user given back access to the data or computer system. It is spread like a worm	Do not open any files from an unknown source Do not click any links in emails Install, run and keep updated a security software package
Rootkit	A rootkit is designed to remotely access or control a computer system without being detected by the security software or the user	An installed rootkit can enable a cyber attacker to remotely access files, access/steal data and information, modify software configurations or control the computer system as part of a botnet	Rootkits are difficult to detect as they are not usually detected by security software Software updates, keeping security software up to date and not downloading suspicious files are the only ways of trying to avoid a rootkit from being installed
Spyware	Spyware can collect data from an infected computer, including personal information like websites visited, user logins and financial information	Usually hidden from a user and can be difficult to detect. It is often secretly installed on a user's personal computer without their knowledge. Some spyware such as key loggers, however, may be installed intentionally to monitor users Can also install additional software or redirect web browsers to different websites. Some spyware can change computer settings, which could lead to slow internet connection speeds or changes in web browser settings	Do not open any files from an unknown source Do not click any links in emails Install, run and keep updated a security software package
Trojan horse	A Trojan horse is a standalone malicious program designed to give full control of an infected PC to another PC	Can appear to be something that is wanted or needed by the user of a PC, or can be hidden in valid programs and software. Trojan horses can make copies of themselves, steal information, or harm the host computer system	Do not open any files from an unknown source Do not click any links in emails Install, run and keep updated a security software package

LO4 Understand the factors to be considered when collecting and processing data and storing data/information

Type of malware	Why it is used	How it works	How to mitigate its effects
Virus	A virus attempts to make a computer system unreliable	Replicates itself and spreads from computer to computer. Can infect files on a network file system or a file system that is accessed by other computers	Do not open any files from an unknown source Do not click any links in emails Install, run and keep updated a security software package
Worm	A worm is a standalone computer program that replicates itself so it can spread to other computers	Can use a computer network to spread. Unlike a computer virus, it does not need to attach itself to an existing program. Worms almost always cause some harm to a network, even if only by consuming bandwidth	Do not open any files from an unknown source Do not click any links in emails Install, run and keep updated a security software package

Botnet An interconnected network of infected computer systems.

Malware Malicious software.

Adware Advertising-supported software.

4.1.3 Social engineering

Social engineering can also take many forms.

Table 4.2 Types of social engineering

Type of social engineering	Why it is used	How it works
Phishing	Phishing tries to get users to input, for example, their credit or debit card numbers, or security details or log-in details into a fake website	Phishing uses a fake website that looks identical to the real one. The most common targets for phishing are bank, building society and insurance websites. For example, the attackers send out emails or SMS that pretend to be from a bank. A link is contained in the email, which the user is asked to click on. This link takes the user to the fake website
Pretexting	Pretexting is when a cybercriminal lies to get data or information	Pretexting usually involves a scam where the criminal pretends to need the information to confirm the identity of the person they are talking to
Baiting	Baiting tries to get victims to give cybercriminals the information they need	Baiting is very similar to phishing. The cybercriminals make a promise of goods to get the information they need. An example would be to promise free downloads of films or music in return for log-in details
Quid pro quo	Quid pro quo tries to disable anti-virus software so that software updates, usually malware, can be installed to gain access to a computer system	Quid pro quo is very similar to baiting, except the promise is that of a service rather than goods. A common method is a telephone call claiming to be from an IT service provider and offering assistance in fixing IT problems
Tailgating/ piggybacking	Tailgating/piggybacking means trying to gain access to a secure building or room	Tailgating/piggybacking takes the form of someone who does not have authority to enter a building or room, following someone who does through the doors. The most common type is an attacker pretending to be a delivery driver and asking an authorised person to hold the door
Shoulder surfing	Shoulder surfing aims to steal data and information	Shoulder surfing is when a person's private and confidential information is seen. For example, an attacker may stand very close to someone using a cash machine in order to see their PIN. This is very effective in crowded places when a person is using a smartphone or mobile device and their log-in details can be seen

4.1.4 Hacking

'Hacking' means finding out weaknesses in an established system and exploiting them. A **hacker** may be motivated by profit, protest or challenge.

There are three main types of hacking that can take place:

- **White hat hacking** is where the hacker is given permission to hack into systems to identify any loopholes or vulnerabilities. As this is done with the permission of the computer system owner, it does not break any of the legislation that relates to hacking. White hat hackers are motivated to keep the computer systems as safe as possible from malicious hacking attempts.

- **Grey hat hacking** is where the hacker hacks into computer systems for fun or to troll but does not have malicious intent towards the computer system. If a grey hat hacker finds a weakness then they may offer to fix the vulnerability – but for a fee! Grey hat hackers can also manipulate the rankings of websites when a search is done on a search engine.
- **Black hat hacking** is where the hacker hacks into a computer system with malicious intent. This intent can include theft, exploiting the data stolen or seen, and selling the data on. Black hat hackers carry out illegal hacking activities and can be prosecuted under UK IT legislation (see Section 4.5, page 62).

> **Common mistake**
>
> Confusing the different types of hackers is a common mistake. Make sure you know each type of hacker, what they do, and why.

4.1.5 Distributed Denial of Service

`REVISED`

Distributed Denial of Service (DDoS) is usually focused on preventing an internet site or service from functioning efficiently, or at all, either temporarily or indefinitely. The attacks usually target sites or services hosted on high-profile web servers such as banks, payment websites (for example PayPal) and mobile phone companies.

4.1.6 Pharming

`REVISED`

Pharming attempts to redirect the visitors from a genuine website to a fake one. This is done without the knowledge or consent of the users. There are some similarities between phishing and pharming. Fraudulent websites are used by attackers carrying out phishing and pharming attacks. Fake or hoax emails are used by phishing attacks.

> **Exam tip**
>
> Make sure you know the different types of social engineering, malware and other threats. You should be able to describe these threats, how they work and the actions that can be taken to mitigate against them.

> **Revision activity**
>
> Copy out Table 4.2, 'Types of social engineering'. Cut up the table to separate the types of social engineering, why they are used and how they work. Mix them all up. Match each type with the correct why and how.

> ### Now test yourself
>
> `TESTED`
>
> 1 Describe **one** difference between baiting and quid pro quo.
> [4 marks]
> 2 Describe the actions that could be taken to mitigate against the risk of a rootkit. [4 marks]
> 3 Explain the motivation of a black hat hacker. [3 marks]

> **Social engineering** The art of manipulating people so that confidential information can be found out.
>
> **Hacker** A person who finds out weaknesses in a computer system to gain unauthorised access.
>
> **Distributed Denial of Service (DDoS)** An attempt to make a computer or network system unavailable to its users by flooding it with network traffic.

4.2 The vulnerabilities that can be exploited in a cyber-security attack

There are three main **vulnerabilities** that can be exploited in a cyber-security attack. These are:

- Environmental
- Physical
- System.

4.2.1 Environmental

REVISED

Environmental vulnerabilities can affect data, information and computer systems.

Natural disasters (earthquakes, floods, hurricanes) could mean internet access is lost, meaning data and information stored on the cloud could be inaccessible. The impact of this could affect recovery from the disaster. For example, data and information may be held by a government about the location and number of people in remote villages. This information could be lost, meaning that any rescue effort may not know how many people to look for.

Computer devices could also be destroyed. A tsunami or flood could destroy or wash away buildings, and if computer devices were in these buildings then they would be destroyed or lost.

Earthquake tremors could damage any hard drive surfaces, causing the data and information stored on them to be unreadable. Backups on physical storage devices could also be affected. Backups stored on the cloud could be inaccessible due to lack of internet access.

Power failures can happen after a natural disaster. No power means devices cannot be charged or may not be able to be used, meaning there is limited accessibility to data and information. Batteries or a power generator could be used as back-up power sources, but there must be fuel available to run the generator.

Lightning strikes can cause a surge or spike in the electricity supply. These surges can affect the operation of hard drives and other storage devices.

4.2.2 Physical

REVISED

Physical vulnerabilities relate to the physical devices used to store data and information, and can also relate to identity theft (see Section 4.3, page 53).

Theft is the most common physical vulnerability. Theft can occur if someone breaks into a building or vehicle and steals the devices, or if devices are left somewhere – such as a train station, on a bus/train or at an airport – and someone else finds them to use for illegal activity. For example, in 2008 a memory stick was found in a pub car park. The memory stick contained passwords for HM Government Gateway, an online system run by the government that allows people to perform tasks such as claiming state benefits and filing their tax return.

System vulnerabilities relate to the running of devices and computer systems, including the use of weak passwords.
System-generated passwords are usually changed to something that the user can remember, such as the name of their dog and their house number. These user-chosen passwords are **weak passwords**, as the simpler the password, the easier it is to guess.

Software must be updated. **Patches** are released to resolve identified vulnerabilities. Updates can be done automatically or manually.

Operating systems and application software can update automatically when the computer system is going through the shutdown process. Any updates that have become available since the last shutdown will be downloaded.

Configuring Windows updates
30% complete
Do not turn off your computer.

Figure 4.1 The Windows update screen

Vulnerabilities Weaknesses that allow an attacker to launch a cyber-security attack.

Weak password One that is easy to find out, or guess, by both people and computers.

Patches Updates released by software vendors for their software.

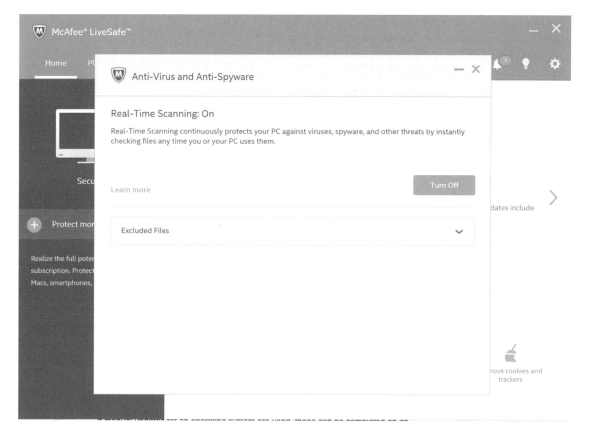

Figure 4.2 Real-time scanning by security software

Security software will update automatically in **real time** because new viruses and other security threats are being released all the time. If an update is found then this is downloaded and installed.

An automatic updating facility means the user does not have to remember to check for updates and the system is kept up to date.

> **Real time** When the computer system is connected to the internet the software will automatically be checking all the time for new updates.

Automatic Maintenance

Windows automatically runs scheduled maintenance on a daily schedule when you're not using your computer.

This includes tasks such as software updates, security scanning, and system diagnostics. This maintenance will run daily if you aren't using your computer at the time you've chosen. If your computer is in use at the scheduled time or maintenance is behind schedule, Automatic Maintenance will run the next time the computer is not being used.

Automatic Maintenance

Run maintenance tasks daily at 02:00 ∨

☐ Allow scheduled maintenance to wake up my computer at the scheduled time

---

Figure 4.3 Settings for scheduled updates

Manual updating can be set to check at a time specified by a user or can be completed on an ad hoc basis. Ad hoc manual updating, however, can be forgotten about and can leave the computer system vulnerable to threats. The problems with manually updating are:

● A patch may not be downloaded as soon as it is released, meaning that the system may be vulnerable to attacks from new viruses.

● The computer system must be switched on and connected to the internet for the update to be downloaded, but the manual update may have been scheduled for a time when the computer system is switched off.

● If updates and patches are missed then the computer system is left open to attacks and threats, which could result in data being lost or stolen.

● Some users may consider the updates intrusive or not appropriate.

● Some users, however, may have decided to manually update the software as they want to look at the updates to decide whether or not to download them.

Some businesses offer Wi-Fi access to customers, but these networks are usually unsecured. This means that no user ID or password is needed to join the connection, which increases the risk of a cyber-security attack.

Insecure hardware can also cause system vulnerabilities. Unsecured devices such as modems, hubs and routers mean that the internet access and the computer devices connected to the Wi-Fi are vulnerable. Data and information stored on the devices could be accessed by a cyber-security attacker.

> **Exam tip**
>
> Make sure you know the different types of vulnerability. You should be able to identify each vulnerability and how it could be exploited by an attacker.

> **Common mistake**
>
> Confusing the different methods of updating software is a common mistake. Make sure you know each method, how it works and why it is used.

> **Revision activity**
>
> Make a list of the different types of vulnerabilities. For each, give an example.

Now test yourself

TESTED

1 What is meant by the term 'weak password'? [2 marks]
2 Describe **one** problem with using the manual update method for security software. [2 marks]
3 Explain **one** impact of an unsecured router. [3 marks]

4.3 The impacts and consequences of a cyber-security attack

4.3.1 The impacts of a cyber-security attack

Every cyber-security attack has impacts. These impacts can affect businesses or individuals, or both.

A **Denial of Service (DoS)** attack can have an impact on authorised users as they may not be able to access the website. The affected business will be impacted as it may lose business or data. For example, if a banking website was the victim of a DoS attack then customers who use that bank's website would be unable to access their accounts, pay bills, transfer money or complete other online banking activities.

Identify theft can also impact on individuals. If personal details are stolen during the attack then the attackers can make a copy of those individuals' details. For example, identity theft could result in big debts being run up, or in passports being issued in individuals' names and possibly used for criminal activity.

> **Exam tip**
>
> Make sure you know the impacts of a cyber-security attack. You may need to identify a cyber-security attack from a scenario in your exam.

Figure 4.4 Stealing personal details means attackers can make a copy of individuals' details

A cyber-security attack can take place on stored data. The data could be destroyed, manipulated, modified or stolen.

- Data destruction is when data is destroyed by a cyber-security attacker and no longer exists.
- Data manipulation is when data is amended to meet the needs of the cyber-security attacker. This type of cyber-security attack is usually found quite quickly. For example, the attacker may change the data in a news feed on social media, which means that false news may be published.
- Data modification also changes data to meet the needs of the attacker. Data modification is very similar to data manipulation, but the attacker usually has different aims. The crime may not be found for a long time. For example, the amount of money in a bank account could be changed. The attacker can then withdraw the increased amount of money, meaning the bank loses money.
- **Data theft** can happen to passwords, personal details and financial data. But it can also refer to the theft of portable storage devices or mobile devices such as laptops and tablets.

> **Common mistake**
>
> Confusing data modification and data manipulation is a common mistake. Make sure you know the difference and can provide examples of each.

The different protection measures that can be used against cyber-security attacks are covered in Section 4.4, page 57.

Now test yourself

TESTED ☐

1. What is meant by the term 'identity theft'? [2 marks]
2. Describe **one** impact of data modification. [2 marks]
3. Explain the impacts of a Denial of Service (DoS) attack on a banking website. [6 marks]

Denial of Service (DoS) A cyberattack where the attackers attempt to prevent authorised users from accessing the service. During a DoS attack the attacker usually sends lots of messages asking the network/servers to authenticate requests that have invalid return addresses.

Identity theft When personal details are stolen and used to commit fraud, for example taking out a loan in someone's name.

Data theft Happens when cyber-security attackers steal computer-based data from a person or business, with the intent of compromising privacy or obtaining confidential data.

4.3.2 The consequences of a cyber-security attack

REVISED ☐

There are three main consequences of a cyber-security attack. These are:

- Loss
- Disruption
- Safety.

Loss

Many cyber-security attacks result in data and information being stolen or corrupted so it can no longer be used. The three main consequences resulting from the loss caused by a cyber-security attack are shown in Table 4.3.

Data subject The person the data is being stored about.

Table 4.3 The main consequences resulting from the loss caused by a cyber-security attack

Financial	A business could lose financial data, such as accounts data. Records of who owes the business money may be lost. Invoices may have to be recreated if the data needed to do this is available
	If personal data has been lost then the business may have to pay compensation to the **data subjects**. This action is required by the legislation relating to the holding of personal data
	The cost of increased security for the computer systems or the business. New hardware/software may have to be bought. Installation and maintenance costs also need to be paid
	The data subjects may also suffer financial loss as the stolen personal details may result in identity theft
Data	Data can be lost and may not have been backed up. This depends on the timing of the attack and the back-up schedule
	There may be a time delay before the data is reinstated, which may have an impact on how a business can interact with its customers/suppliers
	Customers' orders may be lost, including those placed online (e-commerce)
	If customers' data has been lost this may result in identity theft
Reputation	The business may not be seen as trustworthy and its reputation may decline
	Customers/suppliers may not trust the business to safely protect their data, so they may move their custom to a different business or stop supplying the business with goods and services

Disruption

Disruption may occur both when the attack is taking place and after it has happened. The three main consequences resulting from the disruption caused by a cyber-security attack are shown in Table 4.4.

Table 4.4 The consequences resulting from the disruption caused by a cyber-security attack

Operational	The operational running of the business will be affected by the time taken to reinstall the back-up data
	The time delay will mean the business cannot function normally, either between departments (internally) or with customers/suppliers (externally)
Financial	Financial consequences can impact the business if customers' data has been lost, as compensation may have to be paid
	Accounts data may not fully show who owes the business money
	Until the data and systems are restored the business may need to function using limited financial data
Commercial	A cyber-security attack can mean the business cannot function normally
	How the attack affects the business will depend on the type of business that has been affected. For example, a retail business could function with limited operational consequences, but a power generation business may be unable to function safely and may have to be shut down until the data and systems have been fully restored

Safety

A cyber-security attack can have devastating effects on safety. The systems that are linked with safety and security are very well protected against cyber-security attacks, with logical and physical protection measures.

The three main consequences resulting from safety and security issues caused by a cyber-security attack are shown in Table 4.5.

Table 4.5 The consequences resulting from safety and security issues caused by a cyber-security attack

Individuals	The use of the internet and Big Data stores means that most businesses, government departments and the armed forces are inter-connected
	An attack on one of these could lead to issues with national security or the infrastructure of the country, possibly posing issues for the safety of the population
	Personal data could be stolen, leading to identity theft
Equipment	This could take the form of a DDoS
	A business could be unable to fully function and individuals may not be able to access the internet to carry out day-to-day tasks such as online banking
	A DDoS may also affect the connected home, as devices use the internet to interact
Finance	This impact can be while the attack is taking place or after it has ended
	Access to financial websites may be denied, along with the financial data of a business being lost
	The personal financial data of individuals may be lost, meaning identity theft and fraud may take place

Exam tip

You need to know about each type of consequence and how it relates to a business *and* to individuals. You will need to apply this knowledge to a given scenario.

Revision activity

For each consequence, identify the impacts. Give an example of each impact.

Common mistake

Confusing the impacts of a cyber-security attack is a common mistake. There are different impacts for individuals, businesses and national security.

Now test yourself

TESTED ☐

1 Identify **two** consequences of a cyber-security attack. [2 marks]
2 Explain the possible financial impact to individuals of the loss of their personal data. [4 marks]
3 Describe **one** operational impact on a business as a consequence of disruption. [3 marks]

Now test yourself answers at www.hoddereducation.co.uk/myrevisionnotes

4.4 Prevention measures

Stored data and information must be protected. Measures can include:

- Physical
- Logical
- Secure destruction.

4.4.1 Physical

Some devices include a **biometric protection measure**. These can be found on:

- laptops
- smartphones
- tablets.

A characteristic of the owner or user will have been stored. When this is used to access the device, it is checked against the stored characteristic for a match. If it matches then access is granted, if not then access is denied.

Businesses can use biometric protection measures to restrict access to rooms.

Other physical protection measures that can be used include:

- Locking doors when rooms containing computer equipment are not in use.
- Using swipe/**RFID** cards or keypads to activate locks.
- Bolting computer equipment to desks.
- Using special pens to mark the postcode on computer equipment.
- Using CCTV cameras.
- Closing windows and blinds when rooms are not in use.

> **Exam tip**
>
> Keep up to date with emerging technologies that can be used as physical protection measures.

> **Biometric protection measure** A measure that uses a person's physical characteristic, for example a fingerprint, eye scan or voice.
>
> **RFID** Radio Frequency Identification tags can use radio frequency to transfer data from the tags to a computer system, for example to allow access to a room.

4.4.2 Logical

Access rights and **permissions** can be set on folders and files. Authentication and usernames and passwords can be used to do this.

Usernames and passwords are a two-part logical protection measure:

- The **username** acts as **authorisation**. This is a unique identifier for a user.
- The **password** acts as **authentication**. This is linked to the username.

Both must be correct before access is granted.

Access rights and permissions can control which folders and files can be accessed by setting different access permissions. Folders and files can be protected by setting the access rights to read-only so that the files cannot be altered.

> **Access rights** Control over who has access to a computer system, folder, files, data and/or information.
>
> **Permissions** A set of attributes that can be set to determine what a user can do with files and folders, for example read, write, edit or delete.

LO4 Understand the factors to be considered when collecting and processing data and storing data/information

Individual documents can have passwords set on them to protect the contents.

Figure 4.5 Protecting a document with a password

Parts of files can have restrictions set, for example a cell or a worksheet in a spreadsheet workbook.

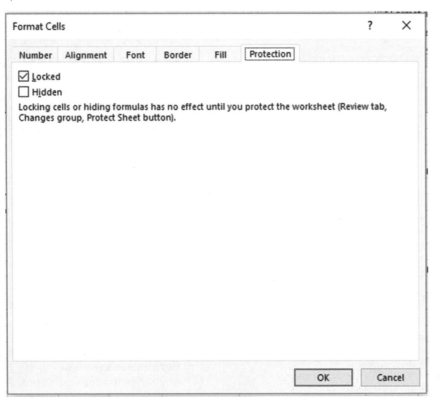

Figure 4.6 Protecting a cell in a spreadsheet

Two-step authentication uses a token to grant access to folders and files.

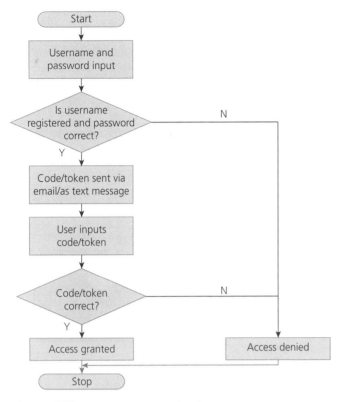

Figure 4.7 Two-step authentication

Anti-virus software detects viruses before they enter the computer system. If a virus is detected then the software automatically quarantines it or asks the user what action should be taken.

Anti-virus software must be kept up to date. When it is bought and installed it is the most up-to-date version. As new viruses are created and distributed all the time, patches will be released to reduce the risk from new viruses.

Automatically scheduled anti-virus scans can be carried out, which search for viruses on the computer that have not been detected by the anti-virus software.

Data encryption software encrypts data so that only users with the **encryption code/key** can read/use the data that has been transmitted. For example, if a user encrypts and sends the phrase:

> The cat sat on the mat

the phrase might be received by the receiving computer system as:

> 5lgP!6n!6K*6lgB!6

Phrases can only be unencrypted if the receiving system has the secret key, which has to be kept secure and accessed by trustworthy people.

Data can be stored/saved in an encrypted form. The secret key will be needed to unlock the data if it is to be used.

Data encryption software Software that is used to encrypt a file or data.

Encryption code/key A set of characters, a phrase or numbers that is used when encrypting or decrypting data or a file.

Secure backups should be made at regular intervals, and kept securely. How often a backup is made will depend on what the data and files contain, for instance:

- A retailer may back up data and files every day.
- Banks and other financial institutions may **back up in real time**.

Backups can be made using portable storage media. The medium used will depend on the amount of data and information:

- Writable CDs/DVDs and USB memory sticks have limited storage capacity.
- Tape drives and extra hard disks are used to store the backups and archives of large companies, but these are very expensive.

Backups should be kept safely and protected from theft or fire. Sometimes the back-up data is encrypted.

The cloud can be used as an online backup. Backups are stored on servers managed by external companies. A charge is made for this, which includes data security and providing the servers. This cost, however, can be much lower than paying for in-house IT technicians to manage and run back-up systems or buying and maintaining dedicated back-up servers.

Figure 4.8 Portable storage media

Exam tip

Keep up to date with emerging technologies that can be used as logical protection measures.

Data needs to be securely destroyed when it is no longer needed or for legal reasons. Data deleted using the operating system software can still be retrieved. Secure methods of destroying data are:

- Data can be **overwritten**. Software is used to overwrite the data with random, meaningless data, usually binary (1 or 0). This is usually used with physical storage devices. The storage device can then be reused.

- A **magnetic wipe** removes the magnetic field part of a storage device. This makes all the data unreadable, but means the storage device becomes unusable.

- **Physical destruction** of a storage device is the most secure, but probably the most expensive, way to securely delete data. The device is so thoroughly destroyed that the data cannot be recovered. This can be done by using:

  ○ a hard drive shredder, which shreds hard drives a bit like a paper shredder

  ○ a drill through or hammer on the storage device

  ○ a steamroller to run over the hard drive.

Figure 4.9 A destroyed hard drive

- Paper-based forms containing personal or confidential data should be securely destroyed. This can be done by using a paper shredder or by burning them.

> **Backup** A copy of the data or files that are currently in use. Backups are made regularly and stored away from the computer system, preferably in another building in a secure place.
>
> **Real-time backup** When a backup is automatically carried out each time a change is made to the data.
>
> **Magnetic wipe** Replaces the data with binary and removes all the basic commands stored on the storage device, making the device unusable.

Now test yourself

TESTED

1 Explain **two** reasons why a bank would back up its data in real time.   [6 marks]
2 Describe **one** problem with using a biometric access device.   [2 marks]
3 Identify **two** physical protection measures.   [2 marks]

LO4 Understand the factors to be considered when collecting and processing data and storing data/information

4.5 Current relevant IT legislation, its implications and applications

4.5.1 Legal protection

Most of the UK IT legislation relates to the protection of individuals, organisations, technological equipment, information and intellectual property.

The main IT legislation you need to be aware of is the:

- Data Protection Act (DPA)
- Computer Misuse Act (CMA)
- Copyright, Designs and Patents Act (CD&PA)
- Health and Safety at Work Act (H&S)
- Freedom of Information Act (FoI).

Important: The details of each Act were correct when this book was published. During your study for this course you must make sure that you know about and understand the most up-to-date versions of each of the Acts, including any changes or additional pieces of legislation that are relevant to IT.

> **Exam tip**
>
> The specification does not list the IT legislation that you should know about in detail. You will need to know about the IT legislation that is relevant when you are studying this course. This means that you need to keep up to date with any amendments or any new legislation that becomes law.
>
> The IT legislation that is covered in this section was relevant in 2017.

The Data Protection Act

The DPA does not actually protect personal data; it protects the rights of the owners of the data. It sets out rules (the eight principles) on how the data should be stored and used by a business/organisation.

The DPA also provides a way for the owners of data to complain and claim compensation if their personal data is misused.

Table 4.6 Key terms related to the DPA

Term	Explanation
Personal data	Any information about a living individual, e.g. facts (such as name, address and date of birth) and opinions that allow the individual to be identified
Data subject	The person the data is being stored about
Data user	The person who needs to access or use the data as part of their job
Data controller	The person who needs to apply for permission to collect and store data. They decide what data needs to be collected, and what it will be used for and how
Information commissioner	The person who enforces the DPA and whom organisations need to apply to in order to gain permission to collect and store personal data. They also make the general public aware of their rights under the DPA

The eight principles are:

1 Personal data must be fairly and lawfully processed.
2 Personal data must be processed for limited purposes.
3 Personal data must be adequate, relevant and not excessive.
4 Personal data must be accurate and up to date.
5 Personal data must not be kept for longer than is necessary.
6 Personal data must be processed in line with the individual's rights.
7 Personal data must be kept secure.
8 Personal data must not be transferred to countries outside the European Economic Area that do not have adequate data protection.

> **Exam tip**
>
> Make sure you keep up to date with any changes in the Data Protection Act and how these will affect business/organisation users and individuals.
>
> You should be able to apply this act to a given scenario and learn the actions that a business/organisation needs to take to comply with it.

Computer Misuse Act

The CMA deals with problems relating to hacking and viruses. Penalties for breaking this law can be a prison term of several years or a fine, or both. The three main parts to this act are:

1 Unauthorised access to computer material.

   This relates to hacking – accessing data or programs that you do not have permission to view. Hacking is illegal only if you do not have permission to access the data or to use the computer to access the data.

2 Unauthorised access with intent to commit or facilitate the commission of further offences.

   If information is accessed, even with permission, with the intention of using it to commit fraud or blackmail for example, then you are breaking this law.

3 Unauthorised acts with intent to impair or with recklessness as to impairing operation of a computer.

   This means that any unauthorised alterations made to computer materials, for example changing files or data, is breaking this law. This includes sending a virus that makes a computer malfunction, alters how it works or damages other data.

> **Exam tip**
>
> Make sure that you understand and can explain how business/organisation users and individuals are affected by the Computer Misuse Act.
>
> Learn the three parts to the CMA and make sure that you are able to apply these to a given scenario.
>
> Keep up to date with any changes to this act and how these will affect business/organisation users.

Copyright, Design and Patents Act

This act was first introduced in 1988 and makes it illegal to copy a work (e.g., a file, image or software) without permission from the owner or copyright holder. Owning the copyright to a piece of work will not stop others from copying it, it merely allows the owner to bring action in the courts.

The main problem is that often the person who copied the work cannot be traced. This is because copies of computer software, images and other digital data, for example audio and video files, are easily made and shared.

People and businesses who break this law risk having to pay a large fine.

The main ICT areas covered by this act are:

● software piracy – the illegal copying or downloading of software

● the use of ICT to copy or download files such as music, video or text, to avoid paying for these – this includes downloading files from the internet

● using software without the correct, or any, software licence

● theft by a business of the methods and ideas of other ICT businesses.

Using software without a licence is the main way in which this law is broken. If a piece of software has been bought by a business with a licence to install it on three PCs but it is installed on the network for all users to access, then the business has broken this law.

If text, images and other files are downloaded from the internet and used, then permission from the copyright holder must be obtained and acknowledged. A fee may need to be paid.

Any copying or sharing of digital files created by others – for example MP3s, DVDs, CDs and software – is a breach of copyright and is illegal under the Copyright, Designs and Patents Act.

> **Exam tip**
>
> As with other acts and laws, you should be aware of any updates to the Copyright, Designs and Patents Act and how these will affect business/organisation users and individuals.
>
> You should be able to apply this act to a given scenario.

Health and Safety at Work Act

Health and safety in a workplace is the responsibility of everyone – employers, employees and visitors.

There are two parts to the legislation regarding health and safety. These are the responsibilities relating to the health and safety legislation (the Health and Safety at Work Act), and the general health issues and physical safety of using computers in the workplace.

The main law covering the use of computer equipment is the Health and Safety (Display Screen Equipment) Regulations:

1 Employers must analyse workstations and assess and reduce risks.

   The computer equipment and the area around it should be safe. If risks are identified then action must be taken to make the area safe.

2 Employers must ensure that workstations meet the minimum requirements.

   Workstations should include tilt-and-swivel screens with enough space for a keyboard, monitor and paperwork. Adjustable chairs and suitable lighting should also be provided for employees.

3 Employers must plan work so that there are breaks or changes of activity.

   Employees should not be expected to work at a computer all day. Regular breaks or a change in the activity that the employees are carrying out should be scheduled into the working day.

4 Employers must arrange and pay for eye tests and glasses if special ones are needed.

   Employees who work with computer equipment can have eye tests arranged and paid for. The eye test can be repeated at regular intervals. The employer will have to pay for glasses only if special ones are required.

5 Employers must provide health and safety training and information.

   Training should be provided to make sure employees can use the computer equipment correctly. The training should include how to use the equipment to minimise risks to employees' health, and the steps that have been taken to minimise the risks.

Physical safety

A safe workplace is the responsibility of employers and of employees. Employees should:

- use the ergonomic equipment – such as chairs, keyboards, mice and wrist rests – provided by their employer
- not drink or eat when using a computer due to possible electrical hazards and possible spillage of food and drink into the computer itself
- not tamper with any cables or computer parts
- place computer equipment safely so it cannot fall or be knocked over
- take care of their own health and safety and that of others.

> **Exam tip**
>
> Make sure you keep up to date with any changes in health and safety legislation and how these changes will affect employers and employees.
>
> You should be able to apply this legislation to a given scenario.

Freedom of Information Act

This act provides two ways for the public to access information held by **public authorities**:

- Public authorities are obliged to publish certain information about their activities.
- Members of the public are entitled to request information from public authorities.

The act covers any recorded information held by a public authority. Recorded information includes any information that is held on printed documents, computer-based files, letters, emails, photographs and sound/video recordings.

The act does not give people access to their own **personal data**. To see this data a subject request under the DPA should be made.

Anyone can make an FoI request to a public authority. It is the responsibility of the public authority to respond.

> **Public authorities** These include government departments, the NHS, state schools and the police force.
>
> **Personal data** Information held about an individual, such as date of birth, contact details, credit reference files or health records.

Exam tip

As with other acts and laws, you should be aware of any updates to the Freedom of Information Act and how these will affect business users and individuals.

You should be able to apply this act to a given scenario.

4.5.2 Ethical and moral issues

REVISED

The internet is a great place to share images, keep in touch with friends and family, and research information. *But,* when using the internet, for example social media, **defamation of character** must be avoided. It is very easy on social media to post comments that are not true. This can also be known as trolling or cyber-bullying.

Trolling is when someone starts arguments or upsets people by posting untruths or cynical/sarcastic comments. Trolling can happen to anyone, not just celebrities. Trolls tend to think, because they are using the internet, that anything can be said or posted.

Another consideration is that of libel. Libel is a written comment that is damaging to a person's reputation. Libellous comments can form part of trolling and cyber-bullying.

> **Defamation of character** When an untrue or false statement is made by one person about another. The statement tries to discredit a person's character or reputation.

Remember

If you wouldn't say a comment to someone's face, then don't post it on the internet.

Common mistake

Confusing the legislation is a common mistake! Make sure you know each piece of legislation and its focus.

Revision activity

Copy out Table 4.6, 'Key terms related to the DPA'. Cut up the table to separate the terms and explanations. Mix them all up. Match each term with the correct explanation.

Now test yourself

TESTED

1 In a business, what is the difference between the data controller and a data subject? [2 marks]
2 Identify the act that should be considered when holding personal details. [1 mark]
3 Discuss how the Data Protection Act tries to protect individuals whose personal data is stored by a business. [10 marks]
4 Explain the meaning of the term 'hacking'. [4 marks]
5 Describe how the Computer Misuse Act (CMA) could be used by a business if a virus was deliberately sent to their computer network. [4 marks]
6 Describe how a business can comply with the Copyright, Designs and Patents Act when purchasing software. [4 marks]
7 State **two** actions that should be taken if a copyrighted image is to be used in an on-screen presentation. [2 marks]
8 Describe **two** actions that an employer needs to carry out to comply with the Health and Safety at Work Act. [4 marks]
9 Explain how the Freedom of Information Act differs from the Data Protection Act. [4 marks]
10 Explain what is meant by the term 'defamation of character'. [4 marks]

LO4 Understand the factors to be considered when collecting and processing data and storing data/information

(4.6) The importance of validity, reliability and bias when collecting and using data and information

Data and information can be collected from a range of sources (see Section 3.3, page 27). Three factors that need to be considered when collecting data/information are:

- Validity
- Reliability
- Bias.

Validity

The **validity** of the source of data and information should be considered. Valid sources include government departments and academic and BBC websites.

Data and information found on a personal website may *not* be valid. **Fake news** is an example of non-valid data.

Reliability

Reliable data and information has a value; the less reliable data and information is, the less valuable it is. Incorrect data and information can be assumed to be wrong, out of date or inaccurate.

It can be difficult to check the reliability of data and information taken from secondary sources. A book can be considered to be more reliable than some websites. Anyone can set up a website and post anything they want on it. The data and information found on a valid website can be seen as reliable, however.

Bias

Information and data that is **biased** may be:

- personal opinions
- statements that have no factual information contained within them
- information that is prejudiced either for or against a person, product or idea.

Examples of ways to spot biased information include:

- Look at who has an interest in a website. If a review for a product is on the manufacturer's website then the likelihood of the review being biased is high.
- If the information is worded very simply or very generalised.
- If the information appears to be based on emotions rather than fact and logic.
- If the information focuses on just one side of the discussion, for example it is very negative or positive.

> **Remember**
> Biased data and information has no value so it is of no use.

Now test yourself

TESTED ☐

1 Describe how fake news could be used on a website.   [3 marks]
2 What is meant by the term 'reliability'?   [2 marks]
3 Identify **two** ways in which to check the bias of a website.   [2 marks]

Validity How believable the data and information collected is.

Fake news Information that has been made up by the people who have written it.

Reliability If the data and information is correct and can be verified.

Bias Considering only one point of view or perspective.

LO6 Understand the different methods of processing data and presenting information

6.1 Selection and justification of the appropriate software tools and techniques to process data

When data has been collected it needs to be processed to meet the defined objectives.

Spreadsheets

One way to process data is using a spreadsheet:

- Spreadsheets are designed to store text and numerical data.
- Graphs can be created to show the results of the processing of numerical data.
- The format of data can be set, for example as currency, to meet the defined objectives.
- Functions and formulas can be used to calculate or recalculate results.
- Modelling can be carried out.
- **Worksheets** can be used within a **workbook**.
- Absolute and relative cell referencing can be used.

Spreadsheet (1) mark = cell
Database (1) mark = Field

Databases

A database can also be used to process data:

- Databases are used to store and process data and text.
- They allow the entry, storage, editing and processing of data.
- A database is stored in a **table** or tables. A table is a file that is made up of **records**. A record is a collection of fields. A **field** holds one item of data. An item of data is made up of characters.
- A **query** can be used to find specific records.
- **Validation** can be set for different fields.

> **Exam tip**
>
> You may need to select the most appropriate software tool that can be used to process data in a given context. Make sure you know the advantages and disadvantages of each software tool so you can select the most appropriate type and can justify your choice.

Table 6.1 The advantages and disadvantages of spreadsheets and databases

	Spreadsheets	Databases
Advantages	Formulas can be used to calculate and recalculate totals	Lots of data, in records, can be stored
	Modelling and What-If investigations can be carried out	Data can be added to or edited if changes are needed
	Worksheets in a workbook can separate different sets of data	Data can be filtered or queried to find relevant results
	The data can be presented as a graph to make spotting trends and patterns easier	Data can be sorted on a specific field
	Data types can be chosen to match the data being stored and processed	A password can be set for security
	Columns and rows can be locked to maintain data integrity	Can be used with other software, for example to send personalised letters
	Can be imported into other documents, e.g. a presentation or report	Validation can be set on fields to minimise input errors
	Can include absolute and relative referencing	Input forms can be created to help with data entry
	The data can be formatted to meet the needs of the audience	Reports can be generated to show the results of the queries
	Can be saved and backed up to prevent loss or damage	Can be imported into other documents, e.g. a presentation or report
	Can be shared electronically	Can be saved and backed up to prevent loss or damage
		Can be shared electronically
Disadvantages	If a model is created the results may not be realistic	Knowledge and skill in databases is needed to set up a database
	Can take a long time to create the spreadsheet	Relationships need to be created if more than one table is used
	Inexperienced users may struggle with the functions and formulas needed	Queries can be difficult to formulate if data from across many tables is required
	If the data is entered manually then errors may be introduced	Security procedures need to be implemented if the database holds any personal details
	An error in the formulas used can affect the results	If the data is entered manually then errors may be introduced
	Not easy to manipulate text	An error in data entry, validation or queries can affect the results produced

---

Revision activity

Copy out Table 6.1, 'The advantages and disadvantages of spreadsheets and databases'. Cut up the table to separate the advantages and disadvantages. Mix them all up. Match each with the correct type of software tool.

Now test yourself

TESTED ☐

1. Describe **two** advantages of using a spreadsheet to process numerical data. [4 marks]
2. Explain how a database can be used to store details about the stock and suppliers of a shop. [6 marks]

Worksheet One spreadsheet contained within a workbook.

Workbook A collection of worksheets.

Table Contains data about 'things', for example students, customers, orders. Each table has a unique name and contains data held in records.

Record A collection of data about a single item, such as a single student or customer. Each record must be unique.

Field An individual data item within a record. Each field has a unique name and contains a single data type.

Query A way of interrogating and manipulating data within a database. A query has rules that filter to find the specific data needed.

Validation Can include length checks, presence checks, format checks, range checks and input masks.

> **Common mistake**
>
> Selecting the wrong software tool for a given context is a common mistake. Make sure you know the differences between spreadsheets and databases.

6.2 Selection and justification of the appropriate tools and techniques to present information

6.2.1 The selection of the appropriate tools and techniques to present information

Can't check if inputting correct data, only sensible data. E.g. Someone's DOB may be 4/12/05 but they type in 7/12/06, the computer won't know. However if a date like 35/12 etc. is inputted, there's no such thing.

REVISED ☐

Processed data needs to be presented. Which tool is used to present the information will depend on:

- what information is to be presented
- how it is to be presented (see Section 6.2.2, page 75)
- the objectives that were defined during the initiation phase of the project life cycle.

Information can be presented using:

- a word processor
- a spreadsheet
- a database
- desktop publishing (DTP) software
- presentation software.

Table 6.2 The purpose, advantages and disadvantages of the different software tools

Tool	Purpose	Advantages	Disadvantages
Word processor	To produce, edit and format documents that are mainly text-based	Easy to correct mistakes Documents can be saved and retrieved later Different versions of the same document can be saved Features can be used to enhance the document Spelling and grammar checkers can be used Document guides are available Data can be imported from other files Mail merge can be used	Files can sometimes become corrupted There may be a limited choice of symbols A device with word-processing software installed is needed to create documents
Spreadsheet	To store and process numerical data	Can store and process numbers Can store text Numbers can be formatted to meet the defined objective Complex calculations can be carried out What-If Analysis can be carried out Graphs and charts can be produced Includes in-built functions	Inexperienced users can input incorrect formula Incorrect formulas can produce incorrect results Not able to process text-based inputs
Database	To store data and records in an organised way	Reports can be created to present results of queries Queries and reports automatically update when data is added Can store data in different tables and reduce duplication Easier to search large quantities of data than in a spreadsheet	Can become complex if several tables are used Can be difficult to set up if the user is inexperienced An incorrect query can produce incorrect results Needs to be kept up to date if the results of queries are to be relied on
Desktop publishing (DTP) software	To arrange text and images into publications	Frames can be used to position text and images Drag-and-drop can be used to place components. Text and graphics can be imported from different sources Software usually includes a range of templates Uses **WYSIWYG**	Different types of DTP software can have compatibility issues Can be difficult to create very precise layouts unless the user is experienced

Tool	Purpose	Advantages	Disadvantages
Presentation software	To create a slideshow to present information to an audience	Slides can include a range of different components

A template can be used to ensure consistency

A slideshow can have links to other resources or files

The show can be presented by a speaker or automatically with no human involvement

Can deliver the message to a large audience in a large space in one go without the need to print anything

Automatic timings can be set for each slide or each element of a slide

A speaker can decide when to move to the next slide based on audience involvement | Too much text on a slide can make the information difficult to read

Effects such as animations or transitions between slides can become distracting

Presentations may become unprofessional if too many features and effects are used |

Exam tip

You may need to select the most appropriate software tool that can be used to present data in a given context. Make sure you know the advantages and disadvantages of each software tool so you can select the most appropriate type and can justify your choice.

WYSIWYG What You See Is What You Get.

Common mistake

Selecting the wrong software tool to be used to present data and information for a given context is a common mistake. Make sure you know the purposes of and differences between each type of software that can be used to present data and information.

Revision activity

Copy out Table 6.2, 'The purpose, advantages and disadvantages of the different software tools'. Cut up the table to separate the purposes, advantages and disadvantages. Mix them all up. Match each with the correct type of software tool.

Now test yourself

TESTED

1 Compare the use of a spreadsheet and a database for presenting numerical data. [6 marks]
2 Describe **one** advantage and **one** disadvantage of using word-processing software to create a business report. [4 marks]

6.2.2 The purpose and suitability of methods of presenting information

There are several factors that must be considered when selecting the method of presenting information.

Target audience

Demographics

Several factors known as demographics must be considered when the method of presenting information is to be selected. Considerations in the selection of the presentation method based on demographics include:

- Gender – Colours may need to be appropriate to male, female or transgender. Gender-neutral colours could be used.
- Age – The presentation method selected, and the content, must be appropriate to the target age group.
- Ethnicity – Ethnicity may affect how the data and information are presented. Numbers are universal, but some audiences may not have English as their first language so text may cause some problems.
- Income – The message or product/service of the information needs to be targeted at the correct income group.
- Location – Where the information is to be viewed and accessed may affect the content of the resource. The location could be internal, external, local, national or international. Location should also be considered if the resource will be viewed online, as some areas have limited 3G/4G or lack fast broadband internet.
- Accessibility – Accessibility can include the information being presented in different ways, for example face to face or via the cloud. Includes consideration of any disabilities, such as providing subtitles for videos or the ability to increase the font size or use a screen reader.

Visibility

'Visibility' refers to how the resource is to be shared.

- 'Public-facing' means the resource can be accessed and used by anyone. This includes the use of a website or information shared at a face-to-face public meeting.
- 'Targeted' means the resource is shared with a specific group of people. This includes emails and responding to requests from social media or the internal staff of a business.

Content limitations

Content limitations are likely to have been defined during the initiation phase when considering the user constraints. They can include:

- the presentation method
- the use of a pre-defined house style
- information, such as contact details, that must be included
- the use of any existing templates
- a word limit on a report.

Availability of information

Real-time data

Real-time data (RTD) is available 24 hours a day and is constantly updated. Applications that use RTD include:

- RTD for transport – such as flights, trains, ships – enables people to plan journeys and check arrival/departure times.
- Satellite navigation (satnav) enables drivers to find a route. RTD can inform them of any delays and of how long a delay is, and can plan an alternative route.
- Smart motorways use RTD to inform drivers of problems and alter the speed limit to suit the conditions on the motorway.

> **Real-time data (RTD)** Data that is delivered immediately after it has been collected.

Figure 6.1 A speed limit on a smart motorway

- Weather data uses RTD to track the progress of bad weather so preparations can be made. The emergency services can use RTD weather data to help plan their rescues and take preventative actions.
- Personal digital assistants use voice commands to access RTD, for example to play music, give up-to-date news briefings, check weather forecasts or answer questions.

Location

Where a person is can affect the accessibility of data and information.

- An unstable or unavailable internet connection will limit access to the cloud.
- Information in a paper-based format will be available only to those who can physically access it.

Delay effects

Any delays in data and information being released will cause issues with accessibility and usability. This may also mean the data and information is out of date.

- Deadlines are set in the initiation phase and must be met.
- Delays in RTD may cause problems, such as:
  - more delays/accidents on a smart motorway if motorists are not kept informed
  - people being unprepared for bad weather, which may cause loss of life and injuries.

What impact is to be achieved from distributing information

What impact is to be achieved from distributing information will depend on the message being given by the information and on the target audience. The impact can be increased by the **distribution channel**. For example:

- A presentation has increased impact if it includes sound, video and graphics.
- Numbers have greater impact if graphs or charts are used to enable visualisation.
- Diagrams increase the impact as they can be easier to understand than lots of text.

How information is shared across distribution channels

There are many distribution channels. Each works in a different way but all enable data and information to be shared between people.

Messaging services

- **Email** can be used across a range of devices as long as an internet connection is available. Attachments can be sent to distribute data and information.
- A post can be uploaded to a **social media** web page. Users can like or dislike a post and share links. A business can use this to keep customers or other interested people up to date.
- An **internal messaging** service is often found on the homepage of an intranet and used to keep the intranet users up to date.

Websites

- **Blogs** are usually written in an informal style. Information can be distributed by the blogger writing about something so that other people can read about it.
- **vLogs** distribute information through videos. The videos can be downloaded and watched or can be watched online.
- The **intranet** can be used if the information is to be kept to a small number of authorised people. An intranet could provide the platform for an internal messaging service.
- **Internet sites** can be accessed by anyone connected to the internet. Most businesses have a website to enable them to distribute information.
- The web pages on an **internal website** can be used to distribute information, provide links to the information or an internal blog, and allow files to be downloaded.

Voice over Internet Protocol

- **VoIP** is useful when the information has to be 'talked through'; files can be sent to the person accepting the call via email.
- Can also be used with video-calling using a webcam, which allows the data and information to be seen.

Distribution channel The methods that can be used by individuals, organisations or businesses to share information.

Blog A regularly updated website or web page that is usually run by one person, the blogger, or by a very small group of people.

vLog A video blog.

Intranet A private network that is accessible only to those people who have log-in, or access, details.

VoIP Voice over Internet Protocol is a system that enables voice calls to be made over the internet.

LO6 Understand the different methods of processing data and presenting information

Multimedia

- Multimedia can be very powerful as a distribution channel.
- It combines elements, for example text, sound, video and graphics.
- It can include user interaction.
- It can be uploaded to a sharing site or embedded into a website or social media page.

Cloud-based

- Files can be stored in the cloud to be accessed as and when a user requires them.
- Requires an internet connection for the data and information to be distributed.
- Large files may take time to download or may become corrupted.

Mobile apps

- Each **app** distributes data and information about a specific thing.

> **Mobile apps** Applications, apps, that are designed to be run on a mobile device such as a tablet or smartphone.

Selection of presentation methods

Which method is selected and used will depend on:

- the defined objectives
- the target audience
- the distribution channel to be used.

Table 6.3 The advantages and disadvantages of different presentation methods

Method	Example	Advantages	Disadvantages
Report	Formal business report	Information about a topic can be collated and presented as a report Headings and subheadings can be used to enhance the structure of the report Graphs/charts can be included	If too much information is included then the user may not read the report thoroughly If the information does not 'flow' then the user may become confused The report must be checked for spelling and grammar errors – these can detract from the message of the report
Presentation	Presentation to customers or focus groups	Slides can include a range of different components, e.g. text, images, graphs A house style or template can be used Links to other resources or files, e.g. a hyperlink to a web page, can be included The show can be presented by a speaker or automatically with no human involvement Audience handouts can be created from the presentation	Too much text on a slide can make the information difficult to read Effects such as animations or transitions between slides can become distracting Presentations may become unprofessional if too many features and effects are used
Graphs/charts	Pivot, line, bar, pie, dynamic	Graphs/charts can help a user visualise the data better Titles and labels can be used to put the data into context Trends and patterns can be easily identified	A poorly presented graph/chart can cause users to misinterpret the data being shown If the wrong data is used to create the graph/chart then the graph/chart can become useless Using the wrong type of graph can make the information difficult to interpret
Tables	To show results	Information can be shown clearly and in an easy-to-understand format Good for summarising data and information	Headings must be used to indicate what each part of the table is showing Cannot provide full details
Integrated document	A document containing components from other documents	Components from other documents (e.g. spreadsheets or images) can be included to enhance the information in the report Graphs/charts can be included to enable users to visualise the information	Some software may be incompatible so components may not display correctly If too many components are used this can detract from the information in the document
End-user documentation	User guide or installation guide	Can help a user use or install a product correctly Can include diagrams to show a user what to do Can be kept and referred to in case of any future problems	Must be written in easy-to-understand language If lots of text is used then the user may become confused Diagrams must be clear and fully labelled or they may be confusing

6.2.3 The advantages and disadvantages of methods used for presenting information

REVISED

When the method for presenting the information is being selected, the advantages and disadvantages must be considered.

Table 6.4 The advantages and disadvantages of each distribution channel

Channel	Examples	Advantages	Disadvantages
Messaging services	Email Social media for business (e.g. LinkedIn, iMessage, Twitter) Internal messaging service (e.g. Moodle)	A wide range of people can be sent or access the data/information The data/information can be targeted to specific groups of people Can be used as a marketing tool to gather feedback Files and images, etc., can be sent/uploaded	Security settings need to be considered Accounts can be hacked, leading to identity theft People can post inappropriate or offensive comments
Websites	Blogs vLogs Intranet Internet	Can be used to get feedback Can be easy to update Alerts can be given when a new post/activity occurs Many people have access to the distribution channel	If not updated then data/information may be out of date The location of the data/information may have to be provided to enable people to access it
VoIP	Skype Lync Podcasts	Free if an internet connection is available Data/information can be sent at the same time as the VoIP call is taking place Features such as call forwarding, three-way calls, call waiting and voicemail can be used	If a stable internet connection is not available then the conversation may lag Each end of the call must have the right hardware and software to speak to one another The quality of the voice may not be good If there is a power cut then VoIP cannot be used
Multimedia	Web conference YouTube	The data/information can be shown or made available to one or many people Links to the multimedia can be embedded on Facebook/Twitter Different elements can be used – sound, text, video, animations Demonstrations can be included, e.g. to show how a product works As the multimedia is easy to change, it is flexible and can be used for many purposes	The message given through multimedia can be lost if too many elements are used If the quality of the multimedia is low, then the message may not be seen as reliable Too much information can be given If the users do not have the correct hardware/software then some elements may not work as intended

LO6 Understand the different methods of processing data and presenting information

Channel	Examples	Advantages	Disadvantages
Cloud-based	Google Drive Office 365	Files are stored off-site so can be used as a backup Access rights can be given so documents can be shared Security can be implemented More cloud storage space can be bought when needed	Must have internet access to be able to download stored files The cloud provider has access to the data and information stored on their cloud storage area
Mobile apps	Travel Fitness	Features can be included in the data/information to increase user interaction Money can be raised if people have to pay for the app Apps can be linked to social media	Apps need to be constantly monitored and updated Regular maintenance needs to be carried out The app needs to be included on app stores or promoted so that people know about it

> **Exam tip**
>
> You may need to select the most appropriate distribution channel and presentation method for a given context. Make sure you know the advantages and disadvantages of each distribution channel and presentation method so you can select the most appropriate ones and can justify your choices.

> **Common mistake**
>
> Selecting an inappropriate distribution channel for a given context is a common mistake. Make sure you know about each distribution channel and are able to select the most appropriate one.

> **Revision activity**
>
> Copy out Table 6.4, 'The advantages and disadvantages of each distribution channel'. Cut up the table to separate the advantages and disadvantages. Mix them all up. Match each with the correct distribution channel.

Now test yourself

TESTED ☐

1 Describe why colour should be considered when creating an on-screen presentation. [2 marks]
2 Explain how an unstable internet connection may affect users accessing data and information stored on the cloud. [4 marks]
3 Discuss how real-time data (RTD) relating to weather can be used by the emergency services. [10 marks]
4 Describe **one** advantage and **one** disadvantage of using multimedia as a distribution channel. [4 marks]

6.3 The resources required for presenting information

It is not only the appropriateness of each presentation method that needs to be considered; the resources needed to use each method also need to be considered. There are three resource requirements: hardware, software and connectivity.

6.3.1 Hardware requirements

REVISED

What hardware is required to view or use the resource will depend on how it is to be presented. For example:

- Report – A paper-based report needs no hardware to view it. But if the report is stored on the cloud then hardware that connects to the internet will be needed.
- Face-to-face presentation – A projector and screen will be needed to view the resource, as well as the hardware the presentation is stored on.

Figure 6.2 What hardware is required to view or use the resource will depend on how it is to be presented

6.3.2 Software requirements

REVISED

Software requirements will depend on the type of resource. A user may need one or more types of software to view a resource. For example:

- Presentation – Presentation software will be needed, but if there are links to other file types then software for these will also be needed.
- **Integrated document** – Word-processing software will be needed, but the components from other types of documents will also need the appropriate software.
- Multimedia resource – Video-playing software will be needed. Some operating systems may include this, but if not users will have to download and install the software before they can view and use the resource.

> **Integrated document**
> A document featuring components from other documents, such as spreadsheets, databases or web links.

6.3.3 Connectivity requirements

REVISED

The requirements to view and use a resource will depend on where it is to be viewed and used and on which distribution channel is selected.

Online storage, such as the cloud or a website, will need an internet connection for access. But if the file size is too big then it may take a long time to download, with the resource **buffering**.

> **Buffering** When the internet connection is too slow to show a resource in real time.

Figure 6.3 Buffering

Exam tip

You may need to consider and select the most appropriate hardware, software and connectivity resources that will be needed to view and use a resource in a given context. Make sure you select the most appropriate resources for the context and can justify your choice.

Common mistake

Selecting the wrong hardware needed to view a resource is a common mistake. Never forget to include the hardware that the resource is stored on.

Now test yourself

TESTED

1 A presentation is to be shown at a meeting in a village hall.
   a   Identify the hardware that will be needed.   [3 marks]
   b   Describe why each hardware device you have identified will be needed.   [6 marks]
2 Identify and describe **two** types of software that may be required to view an integrated document.   [6 marks]
3 Describe **one** problem that may occur when a resource is to be downloaded from the cloud.   [2 marks]

LO6 Understand the different methods of processing data and presenting information

Exam technique

The exam for R012 lasts for 1 hour 45 mins and is worth a total of 80 marks.

This may sound like a long time, but it goes very quickly when you are doing an exam.

This section shows you the different types of questions that may be included in your exam and provides some hints and tips about how to cope during the exam.

Figure 7.1 How to cope during the exam

Types of exam questions and how to answer them

All exam questions use a keyword, such as 'Identify' or 'Describe'. You must recognise these, as these words determine what you are required to do to be awarded the allocated marks.

The main keywords used are listed below, along with a sample question that uses each. The allocated marks are shown in brackets [ ] at the end of the answer lines.

State, Give, Identify

You should answer these questions with a single word or phrase.

Identify **one** input into the evaluation phase. [1]

The answer could be one from:

- Deliverable product (1)
- Test results (1)

Note how the word **one** is in bold; this is to tell you how many answers are needed.

Describe

This keyword is moving to a higher level of difficulty. These answers are usually allocated 2 marks, but sometimes more. If a context is given in the question, you need to provide an answer that matches that context.

> Describe **one** characteristic of data. [2]

The answer could include:

- Data has no meaning (1)
- Data is raw facts and figures (1) before they have been processed (1)
- Data can be made up of letters, numbers, symbols, graphics and/or sound (1)

Remember the '**one**' is in bold, so you need to provide one characteristic in your answer.

Identify and describe, Identify and justify

These keywords are asking you to do two steps in your answer. The first step is to identify, with the second step being to describe or justify what you have just identified.

You need to provide a correct identification before you can be considered for the marks allocated for the rest of the question.

> Identify and describe **one** type of malware. [3]

The answer could include:

- A bug (1st mark) is a software flaw (1) that produces an unwanted outcome (1)
- Ransomware (1st mark) holds a computer system captive (1) and demands money to release it (1)
- A Trojan horse (1st mark) is a standalone malicious program (1) designed to give full control of an infected PC to another PC (1)

There are other sensible answers that could be accepted.

If you look at the answers you will see that the 1st marks are noted. These marks are for the identification of the malware. Remember, without being awarded this mark, you will not be able to be awarded the other 2 marks allocated to the question.

Remember the **one** is in bold, so you need to identify and describe one type of malware in your answer.

Explain

This keyword is moving to a higher level of difficulty than a 'Describe' question. These answers are usually allocated 3 marks, but sometimes more. If a context is given in the question, you need to provide an answer that matches that context.

> Explain **two** effects for people that could occur as a result of a delay in the availability of weather information. [6]

Remember, the **two** is in bold so you need to provide two effects in your answer.

The answer could include:

- People may be unaware (1) of the severity of a storm (1) so may not be prepared (1)
- Emergency services (1) may not have enough staff on duty (1) to help people and keep people safe (1)
- Transport providers (1) may not have made plans, so people could be stuck on trains/buses (1) as the routes may be blocked (1)
- If snow is forecast (1) councils may not have gritted the roads (1) so accidents may happen (1)

There are other sensible answers that could be accepted.

Discuss

This keyword requires you to write an essay. This should be written in continuous prose; writing a list will limit the marks an examiner can award you.

Discuss how access rights and permissions could be used to protect computer systems, files and folders. [10]

The answer could include:

- Access rights are based on the username and password of a user.
- Groups can be set up based on the usernames.
- Permissions are set based on the username.
- Permissions include read, write, edit and delete.
- Files and folders can have permissions set.
- Read-only permissions can be set on files and folders so the contents cannot be altered.

There are other sensible answers that could be accepted.

Compare

For this keyword you need to write about two ways of dealing with a situation. You need to describe the good and bad features of each alternative.

The most common mistake on 'Compare' questions is to write about one of the alternatives in one paragraph and the second alternative in a different paragraph. To be awarded the marks available it must be clear that you have made comparisons. Use words such as 'however', 'and' and 'but' to do this.

A poster advertising a music event needs to be created.

Compare the use of word processing and DTP software for this task. [8]

The answer could include:

- DTP software includes frames so that the different components can be placed in a specific place on the poster. In contrast, word processing software has guides that mean the components may not be placed exactly where the creator wants them.
- Templates are available in DTP and word-processing software, but the templates included in DTP software would be more appropriate for creating a poster.
- DTP software uses WYSIWYG so the poster on the screen will be seen exactly as it would be printed out. Word-processing software can sometimes print out documents slightly differently to how they appear on screen.

There are other sensible answers that would be accepted.

Common mistake

Do not simply answer a question with 'quicker', 'cheaper', 'easier'.

These words must be expanded to provide details. For example, 'easier for a novice user to create a document' may be awarded marks, but 'easier' on its own would not!

In the examination

There are some techniques that you could use in the examination room to help you do the best you can.

- Read the whole paper, checking both sides of the page so that you don't miss anything.
- Make sure that the examiner will be able to read your handwriting. If the examiner cannot read your answer then they cannot award you marks.
- One mark per minute – if a question is worth 2 marks then do not spend more than 2 minutes writing the answer. If too much time is spent on the first part of the exam then later questions will be rushed and marks lost because time has been wasted.
- Focus on the question you are answering – forget the last question. Concentrate on reading the current question and structuring the best answer you can to match the keyword. Some candidates go wrong in a question and this disturbs their concentration for several more questions. Try to focus and forget!
- Take that extra bit of time to think about your answer before you start to write.
- If you do need to cross anything out, be organised. Use a single line and then calmly write a second answer.
- Always carefully read what you have written – is it exactly what you need to say? The words used and their order can make a difference, so take care. You need every mark.

A last note

Examiners are nice people who would like to give you the marks, but they cannot read your mind! As you write your answers, think about what the examiners will read from your response.

Practice questions and commentary

LO1

> 1 A project will be completed using the project life cycle.
>
>   Identify the first **two** phases of the project life cycle.

Mark scheme and additional guidance

Expected answers	Marks	Additional guidance
Initiation	2	Two required
Planning		1 mark each

Candidate answer

Planning

Initiation

Commentary

Question context/content/style

Identification of first two phases of project life cycle. 2 marks.

Requirements

Correct identification of first two stages.

Marks awarded and rationale

2/2

Both phases of life cycle identified.

The order of the answers is irrelevant as the question does not require the phases in order.

> 2 Interaction occurs between the phases of the project life cycle.
>
>   Explain how the phases interact.

Mark scheme and additional guidance

Expected answers	Marks	Additional guidance
The output from a phase forms the input to the next stage	6	
There is no interaction between the evaluation phase and the initiation phase		

Candidate answer

Each phase interacts with the phase that comes after it. The output from a phase is the input to the next phase. This does not happen between the evaluation phase and the initiation phase.

Commentary

Question context/content/style

Explanation of how the phases interact, with consideration of the lack of interaction between the evaluation and initiation phases. 6 marks.

Requirements

Correct explanation of the interaction.

Marks awarded and rationale

6/6

The initial sentence is acceptable for the 3 awarded marks. The second sentence, although the 3 marks can be awarded, could have been more specific instead of saying 'This does not happen'.

> 3 Identify and describe **two** user constraints.

Mark scheme and additional guidance

Expected answers	Marks	Additional guidance
Timescale – the start and end date for the project	6	The identification mark must be awarded before the 2 marks for the description can be considered
Budget – the amount of money that can be spent during the project		
Hardware – the hardware that the client wants the deliverable product to be installed on or run on		3 marks per identification and description
Software – the software that the client wants the deliverable product to run on		

Candidate answer

The start and end date of the project.

Budget is a user constraint. This is how much money can be spent during the creation of the product.

Commentary

Question context/content/style

Identification and description of two constraints that can be defined by the user. 6 marks.

Requirements

Two constraints identified, each with further description.

Marks awarded and rationale

3/6

The initial sentence fails to identify the user constraint and, although the description is correct for timescale, it cannot be awarded any marks.

The second sentence correctly identifies a user constraint. The description can be awarded 2 further marks.

4 A mind map can be used when planning a project.

Describe **two** advantages and **one** disadvantage of using a mind map.

Mark scheme and additional guidance

Expected answers	Marks	Additional guidance
Advantages could include: • Easy to add ideas/tasks at any time • Can help focus on the tasks • Defines the links between the tasks to show dependent tasks Disadvantages could include: • Does not show time for each task so cannot be used to define time schedule • Does not show concurrent tasks, only dependent tasks	6	Two advantages One disadvantage 2 marks each

Candidate answer

A mind map breaks a project down into tasks that have to be completed. The tasks are linked.

Time is not shown on a mind map so it can be difficult to see how long the project will take.

Commentary

Question context/content/style

Description of two advantages and one disadvantage of the use of mind maps as a planning tool. 6 marks.

Requirements

Two advantages and one disadvantage described.

Marks awarded and rationale

2/6

The initial paragraph attempts to describe the advantages. One mark could be awarded for stating that tasks can be linked. There is no indication of how these tasks can be linked, which would have gained an extra mark.

The second paragraph makes some reference to time, so 1 mark can be awarded. But there is no indication of each task having time allocated.

1 Data can be stored and processed.

Define the term 'data'.

Mark scheme and additional guidance

Expected answers	Marks	Additional guidance
Data is raw facts and figures before they have been processed	2	

Candidate answer

Data doesn't mean anything. It is just facts and figures.

Commentary

Question context/content/style

Definition of the term 'data'. 2 marks.

Requirements

A complete definition given.

Marks awarded and rationale

1/2

The answer makes no reference to the fact that no processing has taken place on the facts and figures.

2 Identify the most appropriate data type for storing a telephone number. Justify your choice.

Mark scheme and additional guidance

Expected answers	Marks	Additional guidance
Text Telephone numbers start with a 0 and may have spaces in them	3	Data type must be correct before marks can be awarded for the justification

Candidate answer

They should be stored as text because they start with a 0.

Commentary

Question context/content/style

Identification and justification of a data type for a given context. 3 marks.

Requirements

Correct identification of data type with a suitable justification.

Marks awarded and rationale

2/3

The correct data type has been identified so the justification can be considered for marks. The answer makes no reference to the fact that telephone numbers may include spaces.

> 3 Describe **two** advantages and **one** disadvantage of using emails as a method of collecting data.

Mark scheme and additional guidance

Expected answers	Marks	Additional guidance
Advantages could include: • The same email can be sent to many people at the same time • The results from the emails can be automatically input into software for analysis/manipulation • Little risk of human error occurring when the data collected is being input into the software Disadvantages could include: • Emails may be diverted into spam/junk folders by the email provider • If the fields/data types are not exactly the same as the fields being used for analysis/manipulation, the data collected may be worthless	6	Two advantages One disadvantage 2 marks each

Candidate answer

Emails are fast and free to send. They can be sent to lots of people at the same time. Emails can go into a junk folder, which means they will not be seen.

Commentary

Question context/content/style

Description of two advantages and one disadvantage of the use of emails as a method of collecting data. 6 marks.

Requirements

Two advantages and one disadvantage described.

Marks awarded and rationale

4/6

The initial sentence does not answer the question. In addition to this, the use of words such as 'fast' and 'free' does not attract any marks unless there is further clarification, for example 'are quicker and cheaper than sending a questionnaire by post'.

The next two sentences could confidently be awarded 4 marks for the advantage and disadvantage described. The candidate has failed to provide a second advantage.

4 Explain **two** reasons why an organisation stores files on a cloud-based storage area.

Mark scheme and additional guidance

Expected answers	Marks	Additional guidance
Answers could include: • The files can be accessed from anywhere as long as an internet connection is available • Less memory is needed to access and work on files stored in the cloud • Employees can work remotely and still have access to the files they need	6	Up to 3 marks for each reason

Candidate answer

Staff who work for the organisation can work from home and still access the files they need for work from the cloud.

The staff will need an internet connection but if this is available then they can get access to the files they need.

Commentary

Question context/content/style

Explanation of two reasons why an organisation stores files on the cloud.
6 marks.

Requirements

Correct explanation of two reasons.

Marks awarded and rationale

6/6

The candidate has explained two reasons why an organisation stores files on the cloud.

1 Quid pro quo is one type of social engineering threat.

Identify and describe **two** other types of social engineering.

Mark scheme and additional guidance

Expected answers	Marks	Additional guidance
Phishing – uses a fake website that looks identical to the real one	6	The identification mark must be awarded before the 2 marks for the description can be considered
Pretexting – involves a scam where the criminal pretends to need the information to confirm the identity of the person they are talking to		
Baiting – the cybercriminals will make a promise of an item or goods to get the information they need		3 marks per identification and description
Tailgating/piggybacking – someone, who does not have authority to enter a building or room, following someone who does through the doors		
Shoulder surfing – when a person's private and confidential information is seen as a result of the attacker standing very close to them		

Candidate answer

Phishing is where cybercriminals make a website that looks exactly the same as the real one.

If you are offered free downloads of music in return for information this is called baiting.

Commentary

Question context/content/style

Identification and description of two types of social engineering. 3 marks for each, 6 marks in total.

Requirements

Two correct types identified, each with a suitable description.

Marks awarded and rationale

6/6

The candidate has correctly identified two types of social engineering and provided a suitable description for each.

2 Identify **two** types of hacker.

Mark scheme and additional guidance

Expected answers	Marks	Additional guidance
Black hat	2	Two types
White hat		1 mark each
Grey hat		

Candidate answer

Grey hat

White hat

Commentary

Question context/content/style

Identification of two types of hacker. 2 marks.

Requirements

Correct identification of two types.

Marks awarded and rationale

2/2

Two types of hacker correctly identified.

> 3 Using an example, explain what is meant by the term 'data theft'.

Mark scheme and additional guidance

Expected answers	Marks	Additional guidance
Answers could include: • Cyber-security attackers stealing computer-based data with the intent of compromising privacy or obtaining confidential data • Data theft can also be committed by stealing portable storage devices or mobile devices such as laptops and tablets Example: • Passwords, personal details and financial data	4	Up to 3 marks for explanation 1 mark for example

Candidate answer

Data theft is when a cybercriminal steals data held on a computer device. This is done so they can get secret data and information about people so that they can commit more crimes.

Commentary

Question context/content/style

Explanation of the term 'data theft', plus an example. 4 marks.

Requirements

Correct explanation of the term with a correct example.

Marks awarded and rationale

3/4

The explanation was appropriate; the word 'secret' has been taken as meaning confidential.

No example was included in the answer so that allocated mark could not be awarded.

4 An online shopping website has suffered a cyber-security attack and customer data has been stolen.

Describe **two** impacts to the customers of having their data stolen.

Mark scheme and additional guidance

Expected answers	Marks	Additional guidance
Answers could include: • Identity theft may occur, which means that the cybercriminals could get passports to be used for criminal activity or the customer may get in trouble with the authorities for something they didn't do • Financial problems, as the cybercriminals can take out loans/overdrafts/credit cards in the customer's name without them knowing • Log-in details may need to be changed so that cybercriminals cannot access websites such as online banks	4	Two descriptions 2 marks each

Candidate answer

Customers will need to change their username and password for the website. If the details stolen are also used for other websites then this can mean that the cybercriminals can access other websites, like the customer's bank, and steal all their money.

If personal details are stolen, then identity theft might happen. This means the customer might get into trouble with the police for something the cybercriminals have done.

Commentary

Question context/content/style

Description of two impacts to the customer. 4 marks.

Requirements

Two correct impacts described.

Marks awarded and rationale

4/4

Two impacts have been described. Both relate to the customer so full marks can be awarded.

1 Spreadsheets can be used to process data.

Describe **two** advantages and **one** disadvantage of using a spreadsheet to process data.

Mark scheme and additional guidance

Expected answers	Marks	Additional guidance
Advantages could include: • Formulas can be used to calculate and recalculate totals • What-If investigations or modelling can be carried out • Worksheets can be used in a workbook to separate different sets of data • The data can be presented in a graph to make spotting trends and patterns easier • Data types can be chosen to match the data being stored and processed • Absolute and relative cell referencing can be included Disadvantages could include: • Can take a long time to create the spreadsheet • Inexperienced users may struggle with the functions and formulas needed • If the data is entered manually then errors may be introduced • An error in the formulas used can affect the results	6	Two advantages One disadvantage 2 marks each

Candidate answer

If formulas are used to process the data, the formula must be right or the results will be wrong. If the formulas are correct then the results will change if new data is added or changed in the spreadsheet.

The data can have different data types, so if the data included currency then the data type can be set to show this as using a £ and two numbers after the decimal point for the pence.

Commentary

Question context/content/style

Description of two advantages and one disadvantage of the use of a spreadsheet when processing data. 6 marks.

Requirements

Two advantages and one disadvantage described.

Marks awarded and rationale

6/6

The first paragraph describes a disadvantage and an advantage of using formulas in a spreadsheet.

The second paragraph describes another advantage.

2 Explain how a text-based resource can be made more accessible to users with a sight disability.

Mark scheme and additional guidance

Expected answers	Marks	Additional guidance
Answers could include: • If the resource was a document, then it could be provided in large print or braille • If the resource was a website, then a feature could be included to increase the font size of the text on the screen • The text on a website could be read out by a screen reader that reads all the text on the screen so that people can hear it without having to read it	4	

Candidate answer

Documents can be provided in large print or in braille format.

A website could include a feature called a screen reader. This reads the text on the website so the user doesn't need to read it.

Commentary

Question context/content/style

An explanation of how a text-based resource could be made more accessible to users with a sight disability. 4 marks.

Requirements

Correct explanation of increased accessibility.

Marks awarded and rationale

4/4

The answer provides a clear explanation of ways in which accessibility to text-based resources can be increased for users with a sight disability.

3 A website is one public-facing method of presenting information.

Identify and describe **one** other public-facing method of presenting information.

Mark scheme and additional guidance

Expected answers	Marks	Additional guidance
Answers could include: • Face to face • This could take the form of a meeting where the information could be presented through a presentation by a speaker, with the information provided in a document	3	The identification mark must be awarded before the 2 marks for the description can be considered

Candidate answer

This could be done in a face-to-face meeting.

The information could be given in a document.

Commentary

Question context/content/style

Identification and description of a public-facing method of presenting information. 3 marks.

Requirements

Correct identification of a method with a description.

Marks awarded and rationale

2/3

The answer correctly identifies the method as face-to-face, so the description can be marked.

The description is limited as there is no indication of how the meeting will be conducted, so 1 mark can be awarded for the identification and a further mark for the description.

> 4 A small business needs to create and store invoices. Identify the most appropriate software for this task.

Mark scheme and additional guidance

Expected answers	Marks	Additional guidance
Spreadsheet	1	

Candidate answer

Spreadsheet

Commentary

Question context/content/style

Identification of type of software for a given task. 1 mark.

Requirements

Correct identification for a given task.

Marks awarded and rationale

1/1

Appropriate software correctly identified.

Glossary

Access rights Control over who has access to a computer system, folder, files, data and/or information.

Adware Advertising-supported software.

ANPR Automatic Number Plate Recognition.

Assets Items such as images or videos to be included in the final product.

Backup A copy of the data or files that are currently in use. Backups are made regularly and stored away from the computer system, preferably in another building in a secure place.

Bias Considering only one point of view or perspective.

Biometric protection measure A measure that uses a person's physical characteristic, for example a fingerprint, eye scan or voice.

Blog A regularly updated website or web page that is usually run by one person, the blogger, or by a very small group of people.

Botnet An interconnected network of infected computer systems.

Box set A complete set of programmes in a series, which can be downloaded and watched one after the other.

Buffering When the internet connection is too slow to show a resource in real time.

Closed question A question with only a set number of answers to be chosen from, for example for 'Can you ride a bicycle?' the answers would be either 'Yes' or 'No'.

Concurrent Tasks that can be completed at the same time.

Contingency time Time in a project plan with no tasks assigned. This is used if tasks are not completed on time, to make sure the project still meets the final deadline.

Data encryption software Software that is used to encrypt a file or data.

Data subject The person the data is being stored about.

Data theft Happens when cyber-security attackers steal computer-based data from a person or business, with the intent of compromising privacy or obtaining confidential data.

Data types A specific kind of data item that is defined by the values that can be stored using it or how the data is going to be processed.

Defamation of character When an untrue or false statement is made by one person about another. The statement tries to discredit a person's character or reputation.

Denial of Service (DoS) A cyberattack where the attackers attempt to prevent authorised users from accessing the service. During a DoS attack the attacker usually sends lots of messages asking the network/servers to authenticate requests that have invalid return addresses.

Dependency A dependent task is one that cannot be started until a previous, specified task has been completed.

Distributed Denial of Service (DDoS) An attempt to make a computer or network system unavailable to its users by flooding it with network traffic.

Distribution channel The methods that can be used by individuals, organisations or businesses to share information.

Duration How much time a task should take to be completed.

Encryption code/key A set of characters, a phrase or numbers that is used when encrypting or decrypting data or a file.

Fake news Information that has been made up by the people who have written it.

Feasibility report Created during the initiation stage and considers each of the questions and constraints. Success criteria and objectives are defined in this report. The report forms the basis on which the whole project should be completed.

Field An individual data item within a record. Each field has a unique name and contains a single data type.

Gantt chart A visual method of showing the proposed timing of each task needed to complete a project.

GIGO Garbage In, Garbage Out.

Green energy The use of natural, renewable resources to generate power.

Group/grouping Several components can be moved as one. A feature usually found in DTP or word-processing software.

Hacker A person who finds out weaknesses in a computer system to gain unauthorised access.

Identity theft When personal details are stolen and used to commit fraud, for example taking out a loan in someone's name.

Information Processed data that has a meaning and is in context.

Integrated document A document featuring components from other documents, such as spreadsheets, databases or web links.

Interaction How the phases link together.

Internet of Things The interconnection via the internet of computing devices embedded in everyday objects, enabling them to send and receive data.

Interviewee The person answering the questions.

Interviewer The person asking the questions.

Intranet A private network that is accessible only to those people who have log-in, or access, details.

Iteration The repeating of a phase. Each repetition of a phase, when amendments are made, is called an iteration. The results of each iteration are used as the starting point for the next.

Logical protection methods Computer-based methods that can be put in place by the development team or the network/systems administrator. These aim to reduce, or mitigate, the risks to data being stored.

Magnetic wipe Replaces the data with binary and removes all the basic commands stored on the storage device, making the device unusable.

Maintainability Future development of the product in terms of the use of emerging technologies or adapting to any changes in the client's business or organisation.

Malware Malicious software.

Milestones A given point in time when a task is expected to be started or completed.

Mobile apps Applications, apps, that are designed to be run on a mobile device such as a tablet or smartphone.

MOOC A Massive Open Online Course is an online course with unlimited numbers of students and with open access via a website.

Open question Allows the person completing the questionnaire to give a detailed answer in their own words.

Patches Updates released by software vendors for their software.

Permissions A set of attributes that can be set to determine what a user can do with files and folders, for example read, write, edit or delete.

Personal data Information held about an individual, such as date of birth, contact details, credit reference files or health records.

Physical protection methods Security methods that are designed to deny unauthorised access to computer equipment, resources or buildings.

Primary research method When the data and information collected is fresh data collected for a specific purpose.

Project manager The person who is in overall charge of the project. They do not carry out any of the development tasks associated with the project but they manage the tasks, people and resources needed.

Public authorities These include government departments, the NHS, state schools and the police force.

Query A way of interrogating and manipulating data within a database. A query has rules that filter to find the specific data needed.

Rank order Requires the person completing the questionnaire to rank a list of items in order, for example from 1 to 10 where 1 is the most important and 10 is the least important.

Rating Requires the person completing the questionnaire to rate items on a list individually, for example from 1 to 10 where 1 is very important and 10 is least important.

Real-time backup When a backup is automatically carried out each time a change is made to the data.

Real time When the computer system is connected to the internet the software will automatically be checking all the time for new updates.

Real-time data (RTD) Data that is delivered immediately after it has been collected.

Record A collection of data about a single item, such as a single student or customer. Each record must be unique.

Reliability If the data and information is correct and can be verified.

Resources The things needed to complete the project. These may include hardware and software and different specialist roles such as programmers and testers.

RFID Radio Frequency Identification tags can use radio frequency to transfer data from the tags to a computer system, for example to allow access to a room.

Secondary research methods Methods that use data and information that has already been collected, for example using a book or website to find out statistics that have already been collected and, possibly, processed.

Social engineering The art of manipulating people so that confidential information can be found out.

Static product A product that doesn't move, for example a CD/DVD/Blu-ray cover, poster or magazine front cover.

Table Contains data about 'things', for example students, customers, orders. Each table has a unique name and contains data held in records.

Validation Can include length checks, presence checks, format checks, range checks and input masks.

Validity How believable the data and information collected is.

vLog A video blog.

VoIP Voice over Internet Protocol is a system that enables voice calls to be made over the internet.

Vulnerabilities Weaknesses that allow an attacker to launch a cyber-security attack.

Weak password One that is easy to find out, or guess, by both people and computers.

Workbook A collection of worksheets.

Workflow Which tasks are dependent on another, which tasks have to be completed before moving on to the next, and which tasks can be completed at the same time as others.

Worksheet One spreadsheet contained within a workbook.

WYSIWYG What You See Is What You Get.